MW01001382

Best Easy Day Hikes Series

Best Easy Day Hikes
Rochester, New York

Randi Minetor

FALCONGUIDES

GUILFORD, CONNECTICUT
HELENA, MONTANA

AN IMPRINT OF GLOBE PEQUOT PRESS

FALCONGUIDES®

TOPO! Explorer software and SuperQuad source maps courtesy of National
Geographic Maps. For information about TOPO! Explorer, TOPO!, and Nat Geo
Maps products, go to www.topo.com or www.natgeomaps.com.

Project editor: Jessica Haberman
Layout: Kevin Mak
Maps: Offroute Inc. © Morris Book Publishing, LLC

Library of Congress Cataloging-in-Publication Data
Minetor, Randi.
  Best easy day hikes, Rochester, New York / Randi Minetor.
    p. cm. – (Falconguides)
  ISBN 978-0-7627-5441-0
  1. Hiking–New York (State)–Rochester Metropolitan Area–Guidebooks. 2.
Trails–New York (State)–Rochester Metropolitan Area–Guidebooks. 3. Roches-
ter Metropolitan Area (N.Y.)–Guidebooks. I. Title.
  GV199.42.N652R636 2009
  917.47'89–dc22

                                    2009018277

Printed in the United States of America
10 9 8 7 6 5 4 3 2 1

Contents

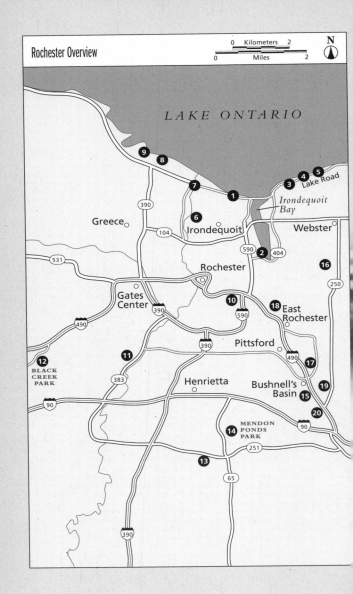

Rochester Overview

Acknowledgments

First, I thank our podiatrist, Dr. Daniel Caiola, whose brilliant work made it possible for my husband and me to undertake this hiking guide and other national park projects.

My hat is off to Scott Adams and everyone at Falcon-Guides whose work brings so many of our books to fruition. To my brilliant agent, Regina Ryan, I am undyingly grateful for all that she does to keep my career on track.

The members of Geneseebirds, the discussion list for Rochester and Buffalo area birders, were generous with trail suggestions and contacts. My thanks to Richard Ashworth, Jim Bailey, Jill Church, Kelly Close, Kathleen Dalton, Steven Daniel, Doug Daniels, Kyle Gage, Jay Greenberg, Allen Handelman, David and Vanna Harding, Kim Hartquist, Greg Lawrence, and Gail Price.

At the Monroe County Parks Department, I thank marketing and education manager T. C. Pellett, director Lawrence A. Staub Jr., and park staff members Brian Needler, Eileen Kennedy, Mark Quinn, Brian Kirchnaler, and Forest Skelton. Stephen Beauvais of the New York State Department of Transportation and Joan Schumaker of the Genesee Valley Greenway also provided useful information. Kathy Blachowski and Gay Mills of the Genesee Land Trust put up with my endless questions and were gracious and helpful. I also thank Dave Schaeffer, trailmaster of the Crescent Trail Association, for assistance above and beyond the call of duty.

Jennifer Centola, Lorraine Woerner-MacGowan, and Gabriel MacGowan joined me to trudge through snow and ice on chill, overcast days. I have so many friends to whom I am grateful, but Martin Winer, Ken Horowitz, and Rose-Anne Moore stand out from this group for their unflagging encouragement and support.

And finally, to my husband, Nic, who walked and rewalked seventeen trails with me, who still likes to read what I write and would hang it on the refrigerator if that would make me happy, I am beyond grateful. I am ecstatic.

How to Use This Guide

This guide is designed to be simple and easy to use. Each hike is described with a map and summary information that delivers the trail's vital statistics including length, difficulty, fees and permits, park hours, canine compatibility, and trail contacts. Directions to the trailhead are also provided, along with a general description of what you'll see along the way. A detailed route finder (Miles and Directions) sets forth mileages between significant landmarks along the trail.

Hike Selection

This guide describes trails that are accessible to every hiker, whether visiting from out of town or someone lucky enough to live in Rochester. The hikes are no longer than 8 miles round-trip, and some are considerably shorter. They range in difficulty from flat excursions perfect for a family outing to more challenging treks in the area's hilly glacial moraine. While these trails are among the best, keep in mind that nearby trails, often in the same park or preserve, may offer options better suited to your needs. I've sought to space hikes throughout the Rochester area, so wherever your starting point, you'll find a great easy day hike nearby.

Difficulty Ratings

These are all easy hikes, but easy is a relative term. Some would argue that no hike involving any kind of climbing is easy, but in the Rochester area hills are a fact of life. To aid in the selection of a hike that suits particular needs and abilities, each is rated easy, moderate, or more challenging.

Bear in mind that even most challenging routes can be made easy by hiking within your limits and taking rests when you need them.

- **Easy** hikes are generally short and flat, taking no longer than an hour to complete.

- **Moderate** hikes involve increased distance and relatively mild changes in elevation, and will take one to two hours to complete.

- **More challenging** hikes feature some steep stretches and greater distances, and generally take longer than two hours to complete.

These are completely subjective ratings—consider that what you think is easy is entirely dependent on your level of fitness and the adequacy of your gear (primarily shoes). If you are hiking with a group, you should select a hike with a rating that's appropriate for the least fit and prepared in your party.

Approximate hiking times are based on the assumption that on flat ground, most walkers average 2 miles per hour. Adjust that rate by the steepness of the terrain and your level of fitness (subtract time if you're an aerobic animal and add time if you're hiking with kids), and you have a ballpark hiking duration. Be sure to add more time if you plan to picnic or take part in other activities like bird-watching or photography.

Map Legend

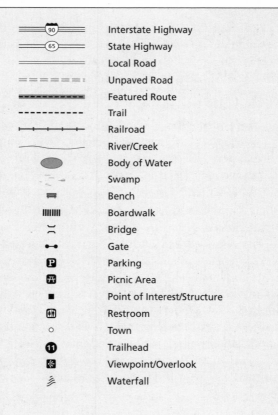

90	Interstate Highway
65	State Highway
	Local Road
=======	Unpaved Road
	Featured Route
- - - - - -	Trail
⊢+−+−+−⊣	Railroad
∼	River/Creek
⬭	Body of Water
	Swamp
⊟	Bench
▥	Boardwalk
⌣	Bridge
•−•	Gate
P	Parking
🛆	Picnic Area
■	Point of Interest/Structure
🚻	Restroom
○	Town
11	Trailhead
◐	Viewpoint/Overlook
≋	Waterfall

Introduction

It's early morning on a hilltop in upstate New York, and as the sun grazes the treetops and penetrates to the forest floor, a chorus of tiny chirrups starts to swell out from behind the oak and maple leaves. In minutes, the hill is alive—literally—with the buzzing of black-throated green and blue warblers, the lyrical calls of rose-breasted grosbeak and Carolina wren, and the wood thrush's almost fairylike song, like music flowing out of a tiny bottle.

Now we can see birds darting from tree to tree, their bright colors turning to fiery reds and oranges in the spring sun. Suddenly, not far from our feet, a rustle reveals an eastern cottontail dashing across our path. In the distance, we spy the triangular ears of a red fox just above the understory, cautiously watching us from a safe interval. Tracks in the soft earth tell us that deer were here as recently as a few hours before, and when we look up we spot an eastern screech owl dozing in a hollow tree, a haven he's frequented for the last several seasons.

Is this a distant mountain wilderness? No, it's Washington Grove in Cobb's Hill Park, in the heart of the city of Rochester. It's just one of dozens of places all over Monroe County where delightful natural surroundings invite a host of gentle wildlife to feed, nest, and thrive—while inviting us all to join in the celebration of our area's unspoiled wilderness.

Not all Rochester residents are aware of the riches our city holds, even beyond its vibrant entertainment districts, cultivated gardens, and architecturally significant residential neighborhoods. Rochester and its surrounding area have been blessed not only with dramatic geological formations and acres of rolling lakeside forests, but also with conscientious landowners, enlightened city, and county management, and impassioned citizens who protect these beautiful places for all of us to enjoy.

Monroe County's ancient history is written in the rock walls of Genesee River Gorge, in the floodplain that flanks the Auburn Trail's Railroad Mills Special Environmental Area, and in the hills—so many hills!—of the Ellison Park Wetlands Complex. Human history abounds along the Erie Canal Heritage Trail, on the Lehigh Valley Trail, and on the Genesee Valley Greenway; and the critical need for nature's survival comes vividly to life in Thousand Acre Swamp, Big Woods, and Corbett's Glen.

If there's a message in Rochester's green spaces and natural lands, it's about its citizens' determination to turn the neglected and abandoned into something beautiful for everyone to enjoy. There are actually more Rails-to-Trails projects in Monroe County than I could include in this book, a testament to our enthusiasm for taking aging beds from America's railroad heyday and turning them into pleasingly long multiuse trails.

If you have not already discovered Monroe County's expansive outdoors, this book will help you select a trail to get you started. Explore the back woods of Perinton or Webster, the hidden glen on the Brighton and Penfield town line, Chili's hardwood swamps as they turn cinnamon and ginger in the fall, or the pristine ponds on Greece's lakeshore. Or venture into the city to hear the dawn chorus at the top of Cobb's Hill, or to see a side of the Genesee River you may not know is there.

Here's a well-kept Rochester secret: Many of the area's

long-distance trails actually connect to one another. A motivated hiker or cyclist could walk or ride from one end of the county to another on a network of well-marked, meticulously maintained trails that extend to provide access to other trails around the state. The Genesee Riverway Trail, Erie Canal Heritage Trail, Genesee Greenway, and Lehigh Valley and Crescent Trails create a neatly woven web of comfortable walkways, reaching out as far as the Finger Lakes Trail in southern New York State.

From the farmlands of Morgan Road in Scottsville to the view from Horizon Hill in Perinton, you're sure to find an outdoor adventure that shows you something new and beautiful about greater Rochester.

Weather

When the annual miracle of spring arrives in Rochester and the city and county burst into bloom, there's no beating this area for the beauty and euphoria the warmer season brings.

The sun shines from 60 to 70 percent of the time from May through August, and idyllic spring and summer days can average in the 70s and 80s, with occasional spikes into the 90s in June or July and cooler temperatures at night. Heavy rains often arrive in June, August, and September, although they rarely last more than a day or two at a time. Rochester has no dry season, so be prepared for rain any time you visit.

To truly appreciate this transformation to the Technicolor spring and summer seasons in Rochester, however, we must face western New York's impressive winters.

Winter temperatures in Rochester average in the low 30s, with significant dips into the 20s, 10s, and single digits in January and February. Check the wind chill before making a winter hike, as the air can feel much colder than the temperature indicates. The annual February thaw can push temperatures into the 50s for a few days, but the cold will return, usually lasting into early April. Snow is guaranteed—an average winter sees 95 inches—and batches of lake effect snow can fall even when the radar shows clear skies. In the winter months from November through January, Rochester sees the sun about 30 to 35 percent of the time.

Fall equals spring in its spectacle, with days in the 50s and 60s, bright blue skies, and foliage panoramas throughout the area's parks and preserves.

Park and Preserve Regulations

You will find the lands listed in this book both accessible and fairly easy to navigate. None of the parks and preserves listed charge an admission fee, so you have free access to any trail you'd like to explore.

While some of the parks have picnic areas with trash receptacles, most of the parks and preserves are "carry-in, carry-out" areas. This means that you must take all of your trash with you for disposal outside of the park. Glass containers are not permitted in any of the parks.

In all cases, dogs and other pets must be leashed. You will see dogs running free in some parks—particularly in Washington Grove—but park regulations and county leash laws prohibit this. It's also illegal to leave your dog's droppings in the park; you can face fines for not cleaning up after your pet.

If you're a gun owner, you will need to leave your weapon at home when entering a Monroe County park, as only law enforcement officers are permitted to carry guns on these lands. Hunting is not permitted in any of the parks and preserves in this book except for Braddock Bay Fish and Wildlife Management Area, although fishing (with a license) is encouraged in many of the parks.

Safety and Preparation

There is little to fear when hiking in upstate New York, whether you're stepping down into the Genesee River Gorge or climbing to the 800-foot summit of Horizon Hill. Some basic safety precautions and intelligent preparation will make all of your hikes calamity-free.

- **Wear proper footwear.** A good, correctly fitting pair of hiking shoes or boots can make all the difference on a daylong hike, or even on a short walk. Look for socks that wick away moisture, or add sock liners to your footwear system.

- **Carry a first-aid kit** to deal with blisters, cuts and scrapes, and insect bites and stings. Insects abound in late spring and summer in Monroe County, especially near wetlands, ponds, lakes, and creeks, so wear insect repellent and carry after-bite ointment or cream to apply to itchy spots.

- **Carry water.** Don't try drinking from the river, streams, ponds, or other bodies of water unless you can filter or treat the water first. Your best bet is to carry your own—at least a quart for any hike.

- **Dress in layers,** no matter what the season. If you're a vigorous hiker, you'll want to peel off a layer or two even in the dead of winter. On a summer evening, the air can cool suddenly after sunset, and rain clouds can erupt with little preamble.

- **Bring your mobile phone.** All of the trails in Monroe County have mobile coverage, so if you do get into a jam, help is a phone call away. (Set it to vibrate while you're on trail, however, as a courtesy to the rest of us.)
- **Leave wildlife alone.** While Monroe County has no resident venomous snakes, bears, mountain lions, or other potentially dangerous creatures, some incidents of raccoons with rabies have been recorded. If you see a wild animal behaving aggressively or in ways that are not typical, leave the area and notify a park staff member or the agency that manages the park or preserve.

Zero Impact

Trails in the Rochester area are heavily used year-round. As trail users and advocates, we must be especially vigilant to make sure our passage leaves no lasting mark. Here are some basic guidelines for preserving trails in the region:

- Pack out all your own trash, including biodegradable items like orange peels. You might also pack out garbage left by less considerate hikers.
- Don't approach or feed any wild creatures (except the birds in Mendon Ponds Park)—the gray squirrel eyeing your snack food is best able to survive if it remains self-reliant.
- Don't pick wildflowers or gather rocks, antlers, feathers, and other treasures along the trail. Removing these items will only take away from the next hiker's experience.
- Avoid damaging trailside soils and plants by remaining on the established route. This is also a good rule of

thumb for avoiding poison ivy and poison sumac, common regional trailside irritants.

- Be courteous by not making loud noises while hiking.
- Many of these trails are multiuse, which means you'll share them with other hikers, trail runners, bikers, and equestrians. Familiarize yourself with the proper trail etiquette, yielding the trail when appropriate.
- Use restrooms or outhouses at trailheads or along the trail.

Land Management Agencies

These government and nonprofit organizations manage most of the public lands described in this guide. They can provide further information on these hikes and other trails in the greater Rochester area.

- City of Rochester Parks and Recreation, 30 Church St., Rochester 14614; (585) 428-6755; www.cityof rochester.gov/parks
- Department of Environmental Conservation Region 8, 6274 East Avon-Lima Rd., Avon 14414; (585) 226-2466; www.dec.ny.gov/outdoor/24428.html
- Genesee Land Trust, 500 East Ave., Rochester 14607; (585) 256-2130; www.geneseelandtrust.org
- Monroe County Parks, 171 Reservoir Ave., Rochester 14620; (585) 753-7275; www.monroecounty.gov/ parks
- New York State Canal Authority, 200 Southern Blvd., P.O. Box 189, Albany, NY 12201; (800) 422-6254; www.nyscanals.gov

- Webster Parks and Recreation, 985 Ebner Dr., Webster 14580; (585) 872-7103; www.websterparksand recreation.org
- The Nature Conservancy, Central and Western New York Chapter, 1048 University Ave., Rochester 14607; (585) 546-8030; www.nature.org

Trail Finder

Best Hikes for Birders

Best Hikes for Water Views

Best Hikes for Panoramic Views

Best Hikes for Fall Foliage

Best Hikes for History Buffs

1 Durand Eastman Park: Eastman Lake Loop

This easy trail follows the edge of a peaceful lake just off the shores of Lake Ontario, reaching a secluded wetland and a glorious orchard and arboretum.

Distance: 1.6-mile loop
Approximate hiking time: 40 minutes
Difficulty: Easy
Trail surface: Dirt path
Best season: April through June, September through November
Other trail users: Cross-country skiers
Canine compatibility: Dogs permitted on leash
Fees and permits: None
Schedule: Open daily 7:00 a.m. to 11:00 p.m.

Maps: National Geographic Topo! New York & New Jersey
Water availability: Restrooms on Log Cabin Road between the Acorn and Maple pavilions, on the east side of Eastman Lake
Trail contact: Monroe County Parks, 171 Reservoir Avenue, Rochester 14620, (585) 753-7275; www.monroecounty.gov/parks
Special considerations: Bring your Yaktrax or other ice grippers to walk this trail in winter.

Finding the trailhead: Take Interstate 590 north toward Seabreeze. Turn left onto Durand Boulevard (this becomes Sweet Fern Road) and continue until the road becomes Lakeshore Boulevard in the park. Pass Durand Lake and continue to Eastman Lake; park to your right, in the beach parking lot. GPS: N43 14.174' / W77 33.462'

The Hike

Durand Eastman Park is just one of the natural spaces George Eastman, inventor and founder of Eastman Kodak

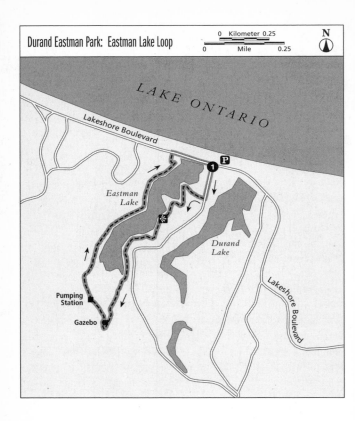

0   Kilometer 0.25

0   Mile   0.25

N

LAKE ONTARIO

Lakeshore Boulevard

Eastman
Lake

Durand
Lake

Lakeshore Boulevard

Pumping
Station

Gazebo

Company, chose to preserve in the early 1900s. He joined his colleague, Dr. Henry Durand, in preserving a total of 965 acres along the Lake Ontario shoreline, adding to the list of generous gifts Eastman made to a growing city in the throes of prosperity.

The bulk of this property is Dr. Durand's former estate, while Eastman purchased adjacent land to make a gift of a total of 5,000 feet of waterfront to the City of Rochester.

In return, the city named the park's two largest lakes after its benefactors.

The walk around Eastman Lake offers the opportunity to see many of the park's varied habitats, from wooded slopes covered in oak and maple trees to a marshy wetland at the shallowest part of the lake. Beyond the wetland lies the meadow that remains from the Durand estate, with orchards of crabapple, cherry, and other fruit trees.

Your walk leads first along the east side of the lake, where you can watch for dabbling ducks—primarily mallards and wood ducks—that visit the lake on occasion. More unusual varieties of waterfowl tend not to frequent the park's small lakes, but migrating warblers fill the trees from late April through mid-May, and again in September and October as passerines make their way across the lake. This park is a key stopover for migrating birds to rest and feed, and they will linger here as they gain strength for the next leg of their journey.

In winter, when snow dusts the hemlock and red pine trees, this trail turns into a frosted fantasy with the lake's frozen expanse broken only by a rabbit's paw prints dashing across the snow-covered ice. Golden-crowned kinglets, cedar waxwings, brown creepers, and downy and hairy woodpeckers all take up residence along this lakeside during the winter, particularly in areas farther back from the park's roads.

As you pass the wetland and come into the meadow, you'll see the beginning of the arboretum planted by Durand in the late 1800s. Apple and cherry trees, magnolias, dogwoods, and many other flowering varieties come together here for a magnificent spring bloom. Today, birds visiting from the Arctic regions often find plentiful food supplies in this park—you may see white-winged and red crossbills, pine grosbeaks, and Bohemian waxwings here in winter. Cedar waxwings crowd these trees in summer and fall.

Best of all, on quiet early mornings, you'll hear the sound of Great Lakes surf pounding the sand and gravel shoreline, even from nearly a mile away at the south end of the trail loop.

Miles and Directions

0.0 Begin the trail on the east (left) side of the lake. Walk up the paved road to the trailhead.

0.1 Turn right and go down the slope to the trail, continuing straight into the woods. At the bottom of the slope, another trail goes to your right; continue straight.

0.4 You've had some nice looks at Eastman Lake, but this spot gives you an unobstructed view.

0.6 Here the lake becomes shallower, and a cattail-filled wetland begins. In the warmer months, keep an eye out for marsh-loving birds like ducks, herons, swamp sparrow, rails, and sora. Golden-crowned kinglets cluster here in winter.

0.8 There's a gazebo here on the edge of the water. The marshy area ends, and a slight rise in elevation creates a meadow. You can cross here, or continue on the trail to the next intersection in about 100 feet, where the trail turns left (joining the Durand and Trott Lakes Trail) or right (to continue around Eastman Lake).

1.0 Bear left and uphill through the clearing here.

1.1 The little gray building to your right is a pumping station, which was used to water the park's former golf course. Not in service now, the station remains a useful landmark as you circle the lake.

1.2 A side trail here goes to the left and uphill. Continue straight along the lake's shoreline. The trail goes around to the right here and then divides, with one path going on into the woods. Go right, toward the road. The trail ends in about 200 feet at Lakeshore Boulevard. Follow the road to the right to reach the parking lot.

1.6 Arrive at the parking lot and the end of the hike.

2 Ellison Park Wetlands Complex: Rifle Range Trail

The least known and most interesting of the Ellison Park trails, this hike winds through rolling, wooded terrain to reach a panoramic view of Irondequoit Creek and its surrounding wetlands.

Distance: 3.4-mile loop
Approximate hiking time: 2 hours
Difficulty: Moderate
Trail surface: Dirt path
Best season: May and June, September through November
Other trail users: None
Canine compatibility: Dogs permitted on leash
Fees and permits: None
Schedule: Open daily 7:00 a.m. to 11:00 p.m.
Maps: National Geographic Topo! New York & New Jersey
Water availability: None
Trail contact: Monroe County Parks, 171 Reservoir Avenue, Rochester 14620; (585) 753-7275; www.monroecounty.gov/parks
Special considerations: Bring your Yaktrax or other ice grippers to walk this trail in winter.

Finding the trailhead: From Interstate 590 North, take the Highway 404/Empire Boulevard exit. Turn right (east) at the end of the ramp. Drive 0.9 mile to the entrance to the Ellison Park Wetlands Complex and park in the parking lot. GPS: N43 10.503' / W77 31.429'

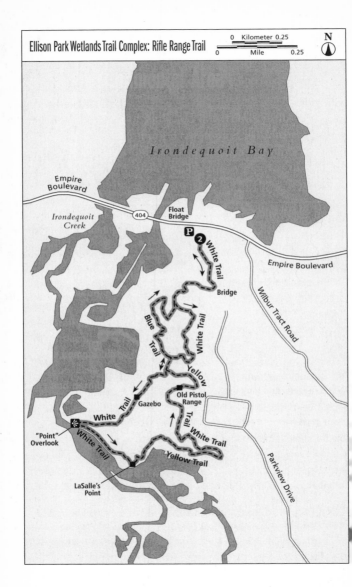

Ellison Park Wetlands Trail Complex: Rifle Range Trail

Irondequoit Bay

Empire Boulevard

Irondequoit Creek

404

Float Bridge

P 2 White Trail

Empire Boulevard

Wilbur Tract Road

Bridge

Blue Trail

White Trail

Yellow

Gazebo

Old Pistol Range

White Trail

White Trail

"Point" Overlook

White Trail

Yellow Trail

LaSalle's Point

Parkview Drive

0   Kilometer   0.25
0   Mile   0.25

N

The Hike

From the parking lot, follow the White Trail blazes as they lead you up a steady incline to a ridge that leads into the wetlands complex. Many color-coded trails crisscross this area; your loop follows the White Trail out to the Irondequoit Creek viewpoint.

As you reach the top of the first incline, notice the water flowing downward to your right. Cross a small bridge over this stream and begin your walk through the wooded hills.

The road noise from Empire Boulevard fades away as you walk deeper into the Ellison Hills, and you're surrounded by hardwood trees gripping gentle slopes, a landscape of dark greens over grasses and ground cover in spring and summer.

The White Trail leads to the edge of this wooded terrain to the south, where it reaches one of the area's most impressive panoramas of Irondequoit Creek and its edge marshlands. This point is known as the Narrows, and it forms the town line between Rochester and Penfield, a spacious area of protected land that extends south nearly to Browncroft Boulevard. You can see the naturally formed levees here along the creek, protecting the surrounding land from potential flooding. In spring and summer, look for long-legged wading birds here as well as several species of dragonfly and lots of butterflies. Canoes and kayaks frequent this waterway on their way to Irondequoit Bay.

Some municipal structures here form a weir. It's likely that this weir will be removed and replaced with a bridge over the Narrows, but the timeline for this is still in discussion.

Turn back and right as you leave the Narrows to follow the creek to the east, continuing to another spectacular overlook at LaSalle's Point. From here, continue on the White Trail until it meets the Yellow Trail, and turn right on Yellow. You'll follow the creek to the southeasternmost point of the trail, at a high point in the Ellison Hills, before heading back on the White Trail, which joins here with Yellow to make this loop.

As the White Trail joins with Yellow one more time, you'll enter the Old Rifle Range, followed by the Old Pistol Range. Used by the National Guard and the U.S. Army for military training until the Korean War, this area was cleared by the Genesee Valley Chapter of the Adirondack Mountain Club to provide a glimpse of the area's past for visitors.

After the Pistol Range, you'll rejoin the White Trail for the last time, retracing your route through the rolling terrain to the parking area.

Miles and Directions

0.0 From the parking lot, follow the White Trail blazes.

0.1 Climb the steady incline to the narrow ridge trail.

0.2 Cross the narrow bridge over the stream. From here, the trail starts to descend back to street level.

0.3 There's a side trail here to the right that provides access to the road; continue to follow the white blazes.

0.5 The Blue and Blue/White Trails join here. Continue to follow the white blazes along the ridgeline, with a gentle drop-off to your right.

0.7 The Blue Trail and the Blue/White Trail cross once again. The blazes are particularly confusing here, so watch for the White Trail blazes on your left. Turn left on the White Trail and follow it as it bends to the right. From here, the trail goes downhill. You'll see the blazes for the Yellow Trail at the bottom of the hill; continue on the White Trail.

0.8 A pair of big pine trees marks a low spot in front of you. Three sets of stone steps lead down into this depression. Stop and explore here, and then continue on the White Trail, to the right. In a moment, you'll see the Red Trail begin to the right; continue straight.

0.9 At the bottom of this short descent, there's a gate to your right. A gazebo is straight ahead. Take the concrete steps up to the gazebo; the White Trail continues behind it.

1.0 The Pink Trail begins to the left—continue straight on the White Trail.

1.2 At the end of this ridge, enjoy the 270-degree view of the Narrows of Irondequoit Creek and the surrounding wetland. The trees thin out here to afford you a sweeping panorama. You'll see a weir across the creek, part of an old municipal water management system. Retrace your steps on the point until you see the White Trail blazes going off to the right and down. From here, you will follow the edge of the wetland with a continuous view of the creek.

1.5 You've reached LaSalle's Point. The Yellow Trail begins to the right, nearly 180 degrees behind you. Turn right and take the Yellow Trail for this part of the hike. This area provides excellent views of the freshwater marsh and Irondequoit Creek. From here, the trail begins to climb.

1.8 The incline ends here at the top of the ridge. Follow the Yellow Trail to the left.

1.9 This is the farthest point into the Ellison Hills on this hike. Rejoin the White Trail here and begin your return, leaving the marshlands for the hills.

2.1 Take a sharp right here at the double white blaze, turn 180 degrees, and continue on the incline. In about 200 feet, bear right on the Yellow Trail.

2.3 Turn right on the Yellow Trail. The Yellow/White Trail crosses here and goes back to the gazebo to the left; be sure to continue right on the return route.

2.4 Here is the Old Pistol Range. Keep following the Yellow Trail ahead.

2.7 Turn right here and go uphill.

3.0 The Blue/White connector trail takes you back to the White Trail here. To return on a different route, turn left on the Blue Trail and follow it down.

3.1 Return on the White Trail to the parking lot.

3.4 Arrive back at the parking lot.

3 Gosnell Big Woods and Big Field Trail

One of the few old-growth woods remaining in the greater Rochester area, this lovely forest combines up- and downhill challenge with tall trees, welcome shade, and remarkable quiet, especially in winter.

Distance: 2.1-mile out-and-back
Approximate hiking time: 1 hour
Difficulty: Moderate
Trail surface: Dirt path
Best season: May and June, September through November
Other trail users: None
Canine compatibility: Dogs permitted on leash
Fees and permits: None
Schedule: Open daily dawn to dusk

Maps: National Geographic Topo! New York & New Jersey
Water availability: None
Trail contact: Webster Parks and Recreation, 985 Ebner Drive, Webster 14580; (585) 872-7103; websterparksand recreation.org
  Genesee Land Trust, 500 East Avenue, Rochester 14607; (585) 256-2130; www.genesee landtrust.org

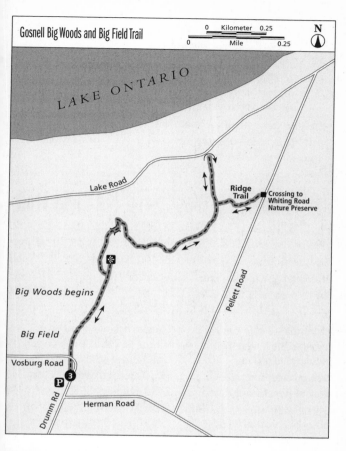

Finding the trailhead: From Interstate 590 North, take the Webster/Highway 104 East exit. Continue on Highway 104 east to the Bay Road exit. At the end of the exit ramp, turn right and drive to Klem Road; turn right. Drive 0.7 mile to Drumm Road and turn left onto Drumm. Continue to the corner of Drumm and Vosburg Roads, where you'll find the parking lot for Big Field and Big Woods. GPS: N43 14.488' / W77 31.429'

The Hike

This special woodland, lovingly tended by the Gosnell family since 1882, has been allowed to thrive with minimal intervention beyond the clearing of a few trails and occasional poison ivy removal. The paths here were worn by generations of neighbors' foot traffic and the hooves of wandering deer, and are only slightly enhanced today with a minimum of marking.

Begin your walk on the edge of Big Field, a wild grassland left undisturbed until after ground-nesting birds have fledged in midsummer. Here native grasses and wildflowers include purple cow vetch, butterfly weed, and common milkweed, while the rest of the plants are invasive—you'll find autumn olive, ailanthus, and black swallowwort among the most prevalent and pernicious species. Lengthen your hike by walking the entire perimeter of this natural field, or simply cross the field on the mowed path to the tree line to enter Big Woods.

Experts estimate that some of the oak, hickory, maple, black cherry, and hemlock trees in these woods are as much as 350 years old, and many have grown to a girth of several feet around, their gnarled roots and well-textured trunks standing in stunning contrast to the younger trees. As you enter Big Woods from the path through Big Field, remember to look up as well as around you to appreciate the heights to which these trees reach. On the forest floor, look for native flowers including Indian pipe, beech drops, and squawroot; double-file viburnum is a particularly showy shrub.

In fall, a veritable party of scarlet and auburn shades emerge in the woods as the leaves gradually change their colors, while winter brings a deep silence broken only by the trickling stream that splits the woodland's valley.

Your hike takes you down between the gentle hills to the floor of the woods, as well as up to the ridgelines that emerged at the end of the last ice age. As you follow the Big Woods Trail and, perhaps, take the side Ridge Trail out to Pellett Road, you'll have the option of crossing the street and entering Whiting Road Nature Preserve. See the Whiting Road Nature Preserve hike to plan a longer trek by taking in this delightful natural reserve and its 3 miles of moderately challenging trails.

Miles and Directions

0.0 From the parking lot, walk north on the mowed Big Field Trail.

0.2 The Big Field Trail goes left; the Big Woods Trail leads straight into the woods. Go straight.

0.3 The Big Woods Trail turns left, and a short trail (200 feet) to an overlook goes straight. Go to the overlook, which provides a view from a high spot of the hills and trees on the east side of the woods. When you're ready, turn around and return to the intersection, and turn right (west) to continue on the trail. You'll go downhill for about 0.1 mile.

0.4 You've reached the bridge over a stream on the valley floor. In about 250 feet, the trail takes a sharp right turn at a signpost. Continue to follow the trail.

0.6 After a long uphill slope, you come to an intersection. Turn left to continue on the Big Woods Trail.

0.8 At this intersection, the Ridge Trail goes to the right. We'll come back to this in a moment; continue straight to the end of the Big Woods Trail.

0.9 The official trail ends here at the End of Trail sign. You can see Lake Road from here. Before you turn around and retrace your steps, take note of the very large tree here at the end of the trail. Naturalists believe that this sugar maple is the oldest tree in Big Woods, with hundreds of years of life to its credit. When you're ready, turn around and proceed to the Ridge Trail intersection, and turn left onto the Ridge Trail.

1.2 The Ridge Trail follows a higher path through the woods, giving you nice views of the rolling hills around you. It ends at Pellett Road. You can cross here and follow the White Trail in the Whiting Road Nature Preserve, which begins here. Otherwise, turn around and follow the Big Woods Trail signs back to the trailhead.

2.1 Arrive back at the trailhead at the Drumm Road parking lot.

4 Whiting Road Nature Preserve

Quiet woods, rolling hills covered with native foliage, open fields, and babbling streams all make this a delicious place for an hour-long stroll or an all-afternoon hike.

Distance: 2.9-mile loop
Approximate hiking time: 1.5 hours
Difficulty: Moderate
Trail surface: Dirt path with some gravel in wet areas
Best season: May and June, September through November
Other trail users: Bicycles, horseback riders, cross-country skiers
Canine compatibility: Dogs permitted on leash
Fees and permits: None
Schedule: Open daily dawn to dusk
Maps: National Geographic Topo! New York & New Jersey
Water availability: None
Trail contact: Webster Parks and Recreation, 985 Ebner Drive, Webster 14580; (585) 872-7103; websterparksand recreation.org

Finding the trailhead: From Interstate 590 North, take the Highway 104/Webster exit. Continue on Highway 104 east to the Five Mile Line Road exit. Turn left (north) at the end of the ramp. Drive to the end of Five Mile Line Road and turn right onto Klem Road. Continue on Klem Road to Whiting Road and turn left. The parking lot for the Whiting Road Preserve appears on the left in about 1.1 miles. The trail begins at the parking lot. GPS: N43 14.819' / W77 28.129'

The Hike

The concentration of varied habitats in a small area makes the Whiting Road Preserve particularly compelling, and the loop trail we recommend leads you through all of them: shrub-seedling and sapling-pole forest, mature woods, a hidden field of grasses and wildflowers, and a third forest with a predominance of beech trees.

From the parking lot, follow the Blue Trail to the left along an easy, level path with wild shrubbery on either side. In short order you'll reach the Orange Trail, and as you turn left, you'll see a creek to your right. This creek and its stream tributaries wind through the entire preserve.

The generally easy path begins to rise and fall as the terrain changes, giving you a sample of the glacially created hills that typify much of the land along Lake Ontario's southern shore. In about 0.75 mile, the wooded area comes to the edge of the south field, an open space thatched with native Kentucky bluegrass and an invasive species called smooth brome. Other native grasses fight for a foothold here, alongside common milkweed, butterfly weed, horsetail, and late summer bloomers like common ragweed and black-eyed Susan. With the addition of alien species that probably drifted here from neighborhood gardens—hoary alyssum, cow vetch, yarrow, and Queen Anne's lace, to

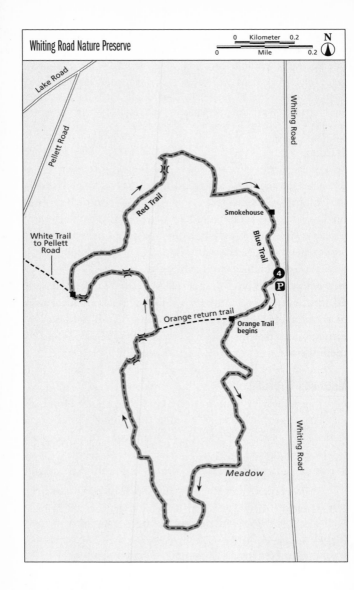

Whiting Road Nature Preserve

0 Kilometer 0.2
0 Mile 0.2

N

Lake Road

Pellett Road

Whiting Road

Red Trail

Smokehouse

Blue Trail

White Trail to Pellett Road

4 P

Orange return trail

Orange Trail begins

Meadow

Whiting Road

name a few—the effect is a rampage of spring and summer color, attracting as many as fourteen documented butterfly species. American coppers can be particularly numerous along the Orange Trail, where sorrel grows just south of the woods.

As you reach the intersection of several trails and begin the Red Trail, the scene around you changes fairly quickly. Here the trail wanders from low spots with Eagle Scout–built bridges over the creek to higher ridges that offer vistas of the terrain. Mature woods surrounds you, creating a particularly striking picture in the fall, and the tap-tap-tapping you hear on a nearby tree could be a pair of resident pileated wood-peckers. A meadow with fruit trees provides feeding ground for cedar waxwings and wintering American robins.

The Red Trail finally bears right, meeting the northern end of the Blue Trail for your walk back to the parking area. As the trees recede, you're back in the shrub-lined passage to the end of the trail; watch for a small brick building—a former smokehouse—that appears just before you reach the trailhead and your car.

Miles and Directions

0.0 From the parking lot, go left on the Blue Trail.

0.2 The Blue Trail meets the Orange Trail here. Turn left onto the Orange Trail. Pass through the woods along a ridge path with a creek bed to your right.

0.4 An unofficial trail goes to the left; turn right on the Orange Trail. Continue through hilly terrain with some gentle slopes.

0.7 Here the woods give way to an open, grassy field. The trail crosses the field and reenters the woods to the left.

1.2 Turn left on the Orange Trail. You'll see a former orchard here as you enter an area of mature woods. Follow along the ridgeline and keep an eye out for woodpeckers. You'll see several trees covered with woodpecker and sapsucker pecking holes.

1.4 Here is the first of several bridges over the creek. Cross the bridge and continue on the Orange Trail. You'll cross another bridge in about 300 feet. Watch for the conjunction of the Orange and Red Trails.

1.6 The Orange and Red Trails meet here, and you'll see a sign for the trailhead as well. You can continue on the Orange Trail and head back to the trailhead and the parking lot, or continue on the Red Trail for a longer loop (another mile). If you choose to loop back, it's about a third of a mile to the parking lot on the Orange and Blue Trails. When you reach the conjunction of these two trails, continue straight on the Blue Trail to return to the parking lot. For the longer loop, turn left onto the Red Trail and walk the long downward slope into the valley of the mature woods.

1.8 At the bottom of the downward slope, you'll reach another Eagle Scout–built bridge over the creek. Notice the scattering of striking white birch among the darker hardwoods around you. There's a cattail-rich wetland coming up on your right, rimmed with beautiful red osier dogwood.

1.9 Here's another bridge over the winding creek. In about 150 feet, the Red Trail turns right, and the White Trail goes straight. Turn right and notice the change in the woodland's character here—conifers begin to dominate the hardwood landscape.

2.1 Green blazes appear here straight ahead. Turn right on the Red Trail. Here the trail descends once again into a lower area, and then begins a fairly steep ascent. It will descend again in about 0.25 mile.

2.5 The last of five bridges crosses the creek here. Shortly, the Red Trail turns right, while an unofficial trail goes straight. Turn right and continue to follow the Red Trail. A break in the woods reveals a meadow with occasional trees, including one large fruit tree not far from the trail. Robins, cedar waxwings, and deer use this tree as a major food source in winter. Keep an eye out for pileated woodpeckers as you reenter the woods on the other side of the meadow.

2.7 Three trails meet here: Red, Yellow, and Blue. Turn left onto the Blue Trail to return to the parking lot.

2.8 The former smokehouse you see here was built in 1904, and was one of several buildings on the property, including the owner's home. When the Gosnell family cleared the other structures, they left the smokehouse as a landmark.

2.9 The loop ends here at the parking lot.

5 Webster Park: West Loop Trail

This short trail through gently rolling terrain offers an ample sampling of glacial moraine covered with healthy woodland, as well as an open field that's a central habitat for birds and other wildlife.

Distance: 1.5-mile loop (2.1 miles in winter)

Approximate hiking time: 40 minutes

Difficulty: Moderate

Trail surface: Dirt path, some paved road

Best season: April through November

Other trail users: Cross-country skiers

Canine compatibility: Dogs permitted on leash

Fees and permits: None

Schedule: Open daily 7:00 a.m. to 11:00 p.m.

Maps: National Geographic Topo! New York & New Jersey

Water availability: Restrooms in the campground near the trailhead

Trail contact: Monroe County Parks, 171 Reservoir Avenue, Rochester 14620; (585) 753-7275; www.monroecounty.gov/parks

Special considerations: In winter, the road into the park is closed; you'll need to walk in to the trailhead (about 0.25 mile).

Finding the trailhead: From Interstate 590 North, take Highway 104 east into Webster. Continue on Highway 104 to the Holt Road exit; take the exit and turn left at the end of the ramp. Drive to the end of Holt Road at Lake Road and turn left. Continue to the well-marked park entrance on the left. GPS: N43 15.468' / W77 27.618'

The Hike

A red fox peering out of the low foliage, pine grosbeaks nibbling on berries high in the trees, a rare varied thrush making a winter stopover on the edge of the lake: All of these happen on or near Webster Park's West Loop Trail, where the park's serendipitous location near Lake Ontario makes it a popular place with birds, small animals, and local human residents. What may seem like a minor trail experience—with a third of the route on open pavement—can turn into a party of wildlife sightings, especially in shoulder seasons when migration, mating, and nesting encourage more ostentatious animal behavior.

The trail traverses a field of low shrubs and open land at the outset, an area that can attract grassland birds, eastern cottontail rabbits, red fox, and deer in the early morning or at dusk. In short order, the path leads into a fragrant spruce forest, quieting the mood and altering your wildlife sightings. Deer are still a possibility, while squirrels, chipmunks, and voles are more likely animals in the trees and on the ground. Keep an eye out for warblers high in the trees in spring and fall, as well as thrushes, waterthrush, and other ground-feeding birds in spring and summer.

A new bridge is planned across West Creek, but it may not yet be in place for your hike—however, the shallow creek is easy to cross by wading or stepping on rocks. Cross the creek and continue into a hardwood forest perched on moraine hills. This is particularly spectacular in fall, when you can enjoy continuous color from early October through mid-November.

As you walk toward the end of the woodland near a scattering of pavilions, you arrive at a side trail that leads into the Whiting Road Nature Preserve. The West Loop Trail forms one end of a continuous trail network, including Gosnell Big Woods and Big Field Trail, that extends along the lakeshore from here to Vosburg Road, about 3

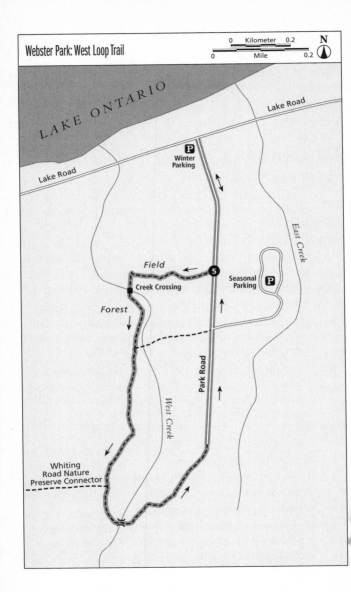

Webster Park: West Loop Trail

LAKE ONTARIO

Lake Road

Lake Road

P Winter Parking

Field

5

Creek Crossing

Seasonal Parking **P**

East Creek

Forest

Park Road

West Creek

Whiting Road Nature Preserve Connector

miles southwest of this park. You may want to consider a shuttle hike that will take you from one end to the other, beginning at this junction and ending at the Vosburg and Drumm Roads parking area for Gosnell Big Woods and Big Field Trail. It's hard to imagine a better way to explore the Webster lakeshore and its carefully preserved woodlands.

Miles and Directions

0.0 In winter, park your car here at the entrance to the closed road, and walk in about 0.3 mile to the trailhead. When the road is open, drive to the trailhead and park in the campground or on the roadside.

0.3 The West Loop Trail begins here. You'll enter a field filled with wildflowers and shrubs, an ideal habitat for all kinds of grassland birds.

0.5 Enter a beautiful spruce forest, which is especially striking when coated with winter snow.

0.6 Cross West Creek here. If the bridge is still out, you can step over the shallow creek on rocks, or use one of the big trees that have fallen over the creek as a narrow bridge.

0.8 Go straight at this intersection. (The trail to the left leads back to the road.) There's a Wegmans Passport Stop here, if you're participating in this fitness program. The trail enters a hardwood forest, which is spectacular in fall.

1.2 Here there's a junction with the Whiting Road Nature Preserve Trail to the right. Bear left. In about 300 feet, a bridge crosses the creek; continue over the bridge.

1.5 You've come out of the woods near the Mohawk Pavilion. Follow the trail to the left, and out to the road. You'll walk down the road to return to your vehicle.

1.7 The trail to the left goes back into the woods to rejoin the West Loop Trail. Continue straight to return to your car, or turn left and back into the woods for a more picturesque walk.

1.8 If you've walked along the road, you've reached the parking area and the trailhead from which you began. If it's winter, continue down the road to your car.

2.1 You've reached the park entrance.

6 Seneca Park: Genesee River Gorge/ Olmsted Trail

Stunning views of sculpted rock walls, ten thousand years in the making, are revealed on this vigorous hike through a park designed by America's foremost landscape architect.

Distance: 4.6-mile out-and-back
Approximate hiking time: 2.5 hours
Difficulty: Moderate
Trail surface: Paved at first, then wood chips, gravel, and dirt path as you go farther back
Best season: April through June, September through November
Other trail users: None
Canine compatibility: Dogs permitted on leash
Fees and permits: None
Schedule: Open daily dawn to dusk

Maps: National Geographic Topo! New York & New Jersey
Water availability: Refreshments available at Seneca Park Zoo; restrooms in the zoo and near Longhouse pavilion on the approach to Trout Lake
Trail contact: Monroe County Parks, 171 Reservoir Avenue, Rochester 14620; (585) 753-7275; www.monroecounty.gov/parks
Special considerations: Optional trails (some steep) into Genesee River Gorge

Finding the trailhead: From Highway 104 West, take the Seneca-Clinton Avenue exit. Turn left onto North Clinton Avenue, and in 0.3 mile turn left onto Collingwood Drive. At St. Paul Boulevard, drive straight across into Seneca Park. Park in the first roadside space available and cross the park road to the metal and concrete stairway that leads down into the river gorge to the pedestrian bridge. This is the beginning of the trail. GPS: N43 11.893' / W77 37.152'

The Hike

What's all the fuss about Frederick Law Olmsted? His name comes up often in upstate New York, but you may not readily connect his name with his extraordinary work—which ranged from the design of New York City's Central Park to the Mariposa Big Tree Grove in Yosemite National Park, California. A master of urban park design, Olmsted created Rochester's Genesee Valley, Highland, Seneca, and Maplewood Parks as a system of parklands, a loosely connected chain of exquisite spaces in the same spirit as his famed Emerald Necklace in Boston. Olmsted's magic lay in his ability to design parks in the middle of congested cities, blocking out the distractions of buildings and noise to provide natural oases in the most unnatural places.

Such a place is Seneca Park, although not many visitors venture beyond the popular Seneca Park Zoo to appreciate Olmsted's creation just to the north. Hugging the edge of Genesee Valley Gorge—the spectacular result of rushing river water carving through solid bedrock, beginning ten thousand years ago at the end of the last ice age—this fairly easy path offers three different access points at which you can descend into the gorge for closer looks at the river's remarkable work.

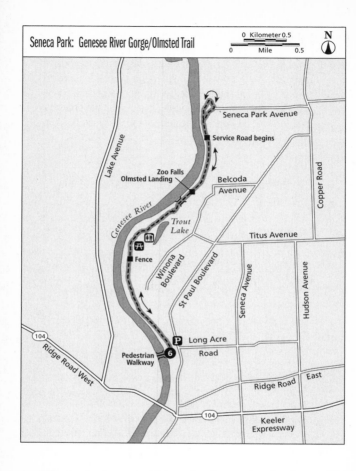

Seneca Park: Genesee River Gorge/Olmsted Trail

0 Kilometer 0.5
0 Mile 0.5

N

Seneca Park Avenue

Service Road begins

Lake Avenue

Zoo Falls
Olmsted Landing

Belcoda
Avenue

Copper Road

Genesee River

Trout
Lake

Titus Avenue

Fence

Winona Boulevard

St. Paul Boulevard

Seneca Avenue

Hudson Avenue

104

Long Acre
Road

Pedestrian
Walkway

6

Ridge Road West

Ridge Road   East

104

Keeler
Expressway

The path also provides a viewing point for Zoo Falls, a pretty waterfall that tumbles down the gorge wall from the park's creek. The falls is best viewed in spring, when snowmelt swells the creek and adds drama to the cascading waters, but it can be picturesque in just about any season, especially after a heavy rain.

Miles and Directions

0.0 Park in the first area with parking spaces along the side of the road. The trailhead is on the west side of the roadway, where stairs (closed in winter) descend to a pedestrian walkway over the Genesee River. This is your first opportunity to enjoy this view of the gorge; take the stairs down to the bridge, and then return to the east side of the river and begin to walk north, up the paved ramp to the top of the gorge.

0.2 The path reaches the top of the gorge. Continue straight.

0.5 There's a fence here with a narrow opening—go through it and continue on the gorge trail. If the opening is too small for you, walk around the fence on the park road and return to the gorge trail.

0.9 Groups and individuals use the picnic pavilions across the road. You're welcome to stop here and rest, or to eat lunch if you're carrying one. The first trail down into the gorge is here.

1.1 The overlook here offers a terrific view of the river gorge. Picnic tables and benches are provided for your viewing pleasure. Trout Lake, to your right, is part of Olmsted's original design for the park.

1.3 Turn right here and take the bridge over the creek. You can also continue along the gorge, but this small shift provides an opportunity to view more of Olmsted's artistry in creating a natural landscape in an urban setting. The trail becomes a gentle but pronounced slope downward, with a railing for easy descent.

1.5 There's another gorge overlook here, well worth the stop. As you continue on the trail, the path crosses another bridge over the creek, and the creek descends sharply into the river; this is Zoo Falls, rushing downward in spring and summer, and trickling delightfully in winter. After the bridge, you'll see a set of steps that lead down into the gorge, taking you to the base of the waterfall at Olmsted Landing. You can descend here for great views, or bear left and follow the gorge trail.

1.6 Here the trail meets the park's service road. If you prefer the flat road surface, continue here to the left. Otherwise, return to the gorge trail.

1.9 The road continues to the right; stay on the gorge trail to the left. You'll cross a trail labeled for cross-country skiing; continue straight along the gorge.

2.1 You've reached the turnaround circle at the end of the gorge trail. Look across the gorge to see Turning Point Park. You can continue straight here and past the circle to reach another path that descends to the gorge, or go straight (downhill) and follow the park trail around the circle.

2.5 Return the way you came to the beginning of the trail. Alternately, walk the service road back to the park's main road, which begins at Trout Lake.

4.6 Arrive where you began, at the parking area and the stairway to the pedestrian bridge.

7 Genesee Riverway Trail: Turning Point Park to Port of Rochester

One of Rochester's newest developed trails, this splendid walk descends quickly from the park to the Genesee River, crossing the river's turning basin on a gently winding elevated walkway.

Distance: 4.4-mile out-and-back
Approximate hiking time: 2.25 hours
Difficulty: Moderate
Trail surface: Paved path and boardwalk
Best season: Spring through fall
Other trail users: Bicycles, inline skaters, cross-country skiers
Canine compatibility: Dogs permitted on leash
Fees and permits: None

Schedule: Open daily 7:00 a.m. to 11:00 p.m.
Maps: National Geographic Topo! New York & New Jersey
Water availability: Refreshments and restrooms available at Port of Rochester, at the north end of the trail
Trail contact: City of Rochester Recreation Bureau, 400 Dewey Avenue, Rochester 14613; (585) 428-6755; www.cityofrochester .gov/parks

Finding the trailhead: From Interstate 590 North, take the Highway 104 West exit. Continue on Highway 104 west to Lake Avenue and turn right onto Lake. Take Lake Avenue to Boxart Street and turn right. Follow Boxart Street around a sharp left turn at the International Paper plant; continue on Boxart to the end at the Turning Point Park parking lot. The trailhead is on the east side of the parking lot, overlooking the Genesee River. GPS: N43 13.646' / W77 37.074'

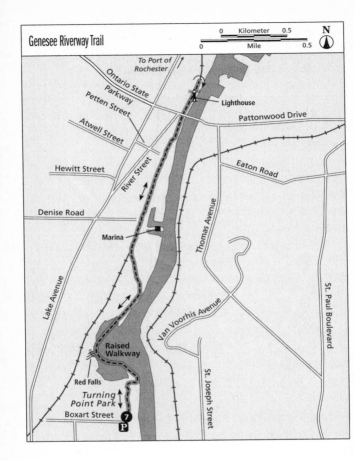

Genesee Riverway Trail

Kilometer 0 0.5
Mile 0 0.5

N

To Port of Rochester

Ontario State Parkway

Petten Street

Lighthouse

Pattonwood Drive

Atwell Street

Hewitt Street

River Street

Eaton Road

Denise Road

Marina

Thomas Avenue

Lake Avenue

Van Voorhis Avenue

St. Paul Boulevard

Raised Walkway

Red Falls

Turning Point Park

Boxart Street

St. Joseph Street

7 P

The Hike

I've chosen the northernmost section of the 9-mile Genesee
Riverway Trail because of its many attributes: It's easily
accessed with plenty of parking, this part of the trail does
not require any walking on city roads, and it follows the

river gorge to the turning point from which the park gets its name.

You'll begin at Turning Point Park, a 275-acre gem loaded with hiking and biking trails of its own. From the parking lot, walk down the paved trail to the 3,572-foot-long elevated walkway that leads through the Genesee River Turning Basin. Since the late nineteenth century, large ships came to Rochester by way of Lake Ontario to load coal brought into this basin by the Baltimore & Ohio Railroad, taking this coal across the lake to Canada. Today this walkway provides close-up views of the basin from just above the water level, giving new perspective and dimension to the river gorge that surrounds it.

Beyond the turning basin, the trail extends into the busy marina area just south of the Port of Rochester. You'll pass the 1822 Rochester Lighthouse (now known as the Charlotte-Genesee Lighthouse), which is open to visitors from early May through the end of October. Much closer to Lake Ontario when it was built, the lighthouse stands in its original spot—but when the city built piers to prevent sand bars from forming across the mouth of the river, the natural deposits of sand created a beach that extended farther out into the lake each year. The lighthouse was deactivated in the early 1880s. It's just forty-two steps to the top, if you're thinking of making a side trip to climb the lighthouse.

When you reach the Port of Rochester building, you may wish to continue walking to view Ontario Beach straight ahead before returning through the basin.

Miles and Directions

0.0 The hike begins at the information kiosk; you can see the paved trail making a long descent from here to the river. Follow the curving trail around the side of the gorge for about a third of a mile, until you're level with the river.

0.3 At the bottom of the hill, you've reached the river basin. The signpost directs you either right to Lake Avenue and the city of Rochester, or left to the Port of Rochester. Turn left.

0.5 You're on a raised walkway that crosses the turning basin, where large ships can turn around after entering from Lake Ontario. As you walk along here, you'll come to Red Falls—look for the falling water directly below the cellular tower.

1.0 Here the raised walkway over the basin ends, and you begin a gentle ascent to street level on a paved pathway.

1.3 To your right, a commercial marina is crowded with sailboats and motorboats in spring, summer, and early fall.

1.7 Cross Petten Street and continue on the trail through the three posts on the opposite side of the street. The paved trail goes on along the river, paralleling River Street.

2.0 You've reached a parking lot and one of the official starting points for the Riverway Trail. The original Rochester Lighthouse is on your left. Continue straight along the path through this busy waterfront area to the Port of Rochester.

2.2 Here's the Port of Rochester Terminal building, where you'll find restaurants, a snack bar, and restroom facilities. Stop here before retracing your steps to Turning Point Park.

4.4 Your hike ends at the parking lot at the top of the hill, in Turning Point Park.

8 Island Cottage Woods Preserve

This short trail ambles through a level, wooded area to the wetland surrounding Round Pond. Located across the road from Lake Ontario, this legendary woods serves as a haven for migrating warblers and other spring passerines, which rest and feed here in spring before their Great Lakes crossing.

Distance: 0.9-mile loop
Approximate hiking time: 30 to 45 minutes, depending on bird activity
Difficulty: Easy
Trail surface: Cleared dirt path with boardwalk sections; wood mulch applied in spring over wet spots
Best season: April through June
Other trail users: Birders
Canine compatibility: Dogs permitted on leash

Fees and permits: None
Schedule: Open daily dawn to dusk
Maps: National Geographic Topo! New York & New Jersey
Water availability: None
Trail contact: Genesee Land Trust, 500 East Avenue, Rochester 14607; (585) 256-2130; www.geneseelandtrust.org
Special considerations: Bring binoculars for peak birding experiences in April and May

Finding the trailhead: From Interstate 390 North, take the Latta Road exit. Turn right at the end of the ramp onto Latta Road and take the next left onto Island Cottage Road. Continue on Island Cottage Road until you see the Lake Plains Waterfowl sign; turn right onto the dirt road. Continue on this road until it ends at a parking area. The trailhead is straight ahead and to the right. GPS: N43 16.445' / W77 39.609'

The Hike

Say "Island Cottage Woods" to local birders, and the words evoke instant smiles and faraway gazes as they consider the

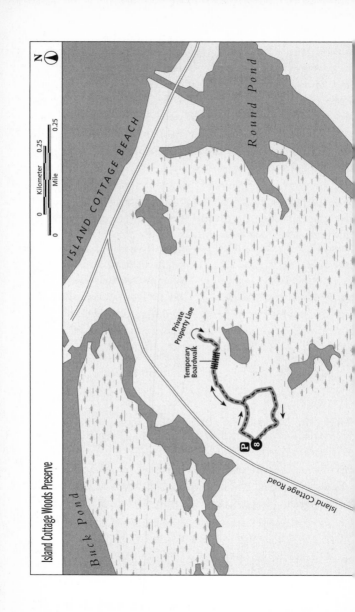

Island Cottage Woods Preserve

N

Buck Pond

ISLAND COTTAGE BEACH

Round Pond

Private Property Line

Temporary Boardwalk

0   Kilometer   0.25

0   Mile   0.25

P

8

Island Cottage Road

number of life birds—bird species seen for the first time—they accumulated in a single morning in this patch of woodland. Spring's migratory fallout here can produce as many as fifteen warbler species at once, as well as vireos, sapsuckers, woodpeckers, thrushes, wrens, and other songbirds.

The walk itself is a pleasant amble along a level, carefully tended path, through land maintained by the Genesee Land Trust. The path is often moist and muddy in late spring, but volunteers arrive in early May to spread wood shavings, while Eagle Scouts participate in boardwalk construction projects that have made this strip of land especially easy to enjoy.

Part of the land here is privately owned, so the Land Trust's blazes disappear before the woods ends. You will see the trail continuing along a narrow corridor near Round Pond, on the edge of posted land, and then straight ahead—this goes into Schaller's Woods, privately owned land that is open to birders and walkers by special arrangement between the landowner and the Land Trust. You are welcome to continue your walk in the woods ahead, but we can't publish the trail map for this part of the preserve.

Begin your walk just past the Lake Plains Waterfowl building at the end of the dirt road. In spring and summer, wildflowers including mayapple, trillium, and violets blanket the ground on all sides of the trail, while small furry animals make their homes beneath the understory. Watch for gray squirrels, eastern chipmunks, and red fox, as well as hermit thrush, wood thrush, and northern waterthrush sorting through last year's leaves in search of bugs. An American woodcock has been known to nest on the ground in this area.

As you approach Round Pond and stand on the edge of the wetland, opportunities increase for sightings of sora,

Virginia rails, green herons, and even bitterns. Wet spots in the woods often attract dabbling ducks, and a scan of the pond can produce pied-billed grebe, mute and tundra swans, many duck species, and herons and moorhens around the edges. In this clearing, scan the skies for migrating hawks passing overhead.

If you're staying with the Land Trust path, you'll turn around shortly and head back into the woods.

Miles and Directions

0.0 From the parking area, pass the guardrail and walk into the woods on the trail. Follow the clearly delineated trail (defined with logs on either side) in an arc through the preserve.

0.3 A spur trail goes to the right here. Turn right.

0.4 The trail comes to a stop here on the edge of private property. You'll see pink and orange tape/ribbon along the edge of the private land; the Genesee Land Trust signs continue to the right. Follow these signs. In about 100 feet, you'll come to a temporary walkway over a wet area; plans are to replace the boards here with a bridge when funds permit. Continue straight.

0.5 Note the wetland to your right—this is Round Pond, a favorite birding spot. Continue to the old-growth tree straight ahead on the trail. This is the official end of the preserve. You may wish to turn around here and follow the Land Trust signs back through the preserve.

0.6 Take the trail to the left to complete the loop back to the trailhead.

0.8 The trail emerges at the road. Turn left and walk back to the parking area on the road.

0.9 Arrive back at the parking area.

9 Braddock Bay Fish and Wildlife Management Area: Beatty Point Trail

On the edge of the Braddock Bay preserve, a level, wide path provides access to Beatty Point, a finger of land that reaches into the pristine, undeveloped Buck Pond.

Distance: 2-mile out-and-back
Approximate hiking time: 1.25 hours
Difficulty: Easy
Trail surface: Former paved road, now mostly gravel
Best season: Spring and summer
Other trail users: Birders, bicycles, anglers, bow hunters, waterfowl hunters, snowmobiles and cross-country skiers
Canine compatibility: Dogs permitted on leash
Fees and permits: None
Schedule: Open daily dawn to dusk

Maps: National Geographic Topo! New York & New Jersey
Water availability: None
Trail contact: DEC Region 8, 6274 East Avon-Lima Road, Avon 14414-9519; (585) 226-2466; www.dec.ny.gov/outdoor/24428.html
Town of Greece Parks and Recreation, 1 Vince Tofifay Boulevard, Rochester 14612; (585) 225-2000; www.greeceny.gov
Special considerations: Wear orange during the hunting season (generally mid-October through mid-December)

Finding the trailhead: From the Lake Ontario State Parkway going west from Interstate 390 North, take the Long Pond Road exit. Turn right (north) onto Long Pond Road and drive a few hundred feet to the paved parking area on the right side of the road. Park here; the trailhead is ahead, southeast of the parking area. GPS: N43 17.019' / W77 41.490'

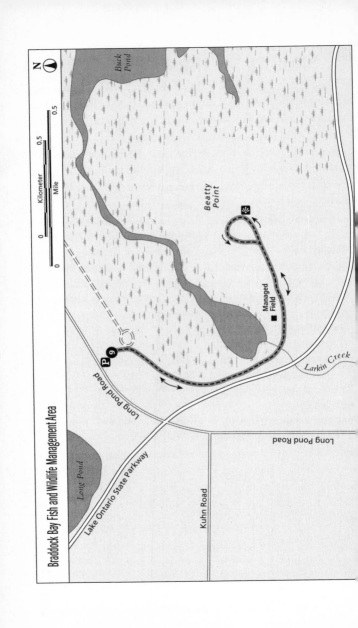

Braddock Bay Fish and Wildlife Management Area

N

Long Pond

Lake Ontario State Parkway

Long Pond Road

Kuhn Road

Long Pond Road

Larkin Creek

Managed Field

Beatty Point

Buck Pond

P 9

Kilometer

Mile

0   0.5   0.5

The Hike

One of five units of the Braddock Bay complex, Buck Pond retains a tenuous but consistent connection to Lake Ontario through many channels that wind through cattail marshes along its shores. Devoid of residential or commercial development, this little lake serves as a safe haven for waterfowl and long-legged waders in spring, summer, and fall, while providing breeding ground for painted turtles and many common species of frogs.

The hike along Beatty Point is the easiest walk in this book, a casual stroll on a wide, level, gravel path through fields of native and invasive grasses—most notably switchgrass, which has taken over much of this land—to a wide view of the pond from the trail's turnaround loop. Here you can search for wood ducks and blue-winged teal, both of which nest here, as well as American wigeons, gadwall, northern shovelers, and northern pintails, all of which may stop here at some point in spring, summer, and fall. Before the pond freezes in winter and as it thaws in early spring, red-breasted mergansers, buffleheads, and long-tailed ducks may appear. Great blue and green herons are resident. In winter, snowy owls sometimes hunt around the pond.

In addition to the thick cattails, you'll find abundant water lilies on the pond's surface by midsummer, and vegetation including swamp loosestrife, burweed, and bulrushes, to name a few. Wildflowers in the surrounding fields can include black-eyed Susans, New England aster, ox-eye sunflower and Joe Pye weed in summer, and goldenrod and asters in late summer and fall.

Miles and Directions

0.0 Leave the parking lot and begin your walk on the wide pathway.

0.6 There's a bridge here over Larkin Creek. In about 350 feet, you'll come to a mowed field—this is a testing area for a DEC project to improve grassland habitat. Mowing here encourages a more diverse selection of grasses to grow, beyond the switchgrass that has come to dominate this property. More variety will lead to a better food supply for native birds and animals.

0.9 Bear right at this intersection, which forms the "throat" of the loop at the end of the trail.

1.0 This picnic spot gives you the best view of Buck Pond. You can see the Crescent Beach Restaurant, Inn and Spa on the other side of the pond. When you're ready, continue to follow the loop around to the left, and begin your return walk on the trail.

2.0 Reach the trailhead and the parking lot.

10 Washington Grove/Cobbs Hill Park

This hundred-acre urban wilderness walk leads to one of the highest points in Rochester, where you'll find the area's best view of the city skyline.

Distance: 2.1-mile figure eight
Approximate hiking time: 1.25 hours
Difficulty: Moderate
Trail surface: Dirt path leading to paved walkway
Best season: May and June, September through November
Other trail users: Some mountain bikes, although this is illegal
Canine compatibility: Dogs permitted on leash
Fees and permits: None

Schedule: Open daily 6:00 a.m. to 9:00 p.m.
Maps: National Geographic Topo! New York & New Jersey
Water availability: None
Trail contact: City of Rochester Recreation Bureau, 400 Dewey Avenue, Rochester 14613; (585) 428-6755; www.cityofrochester .gov/parks
Special considerations: There are many cross trails here and no blazes or trail names.

Finding the trailhead: From Interstate 590 North, take the Highland Avenue exit. Turn left at the end of the ramp. Drive on Highland Avenue past Winton Road, Cobbs Hill Drive, and Highland Heights. The next right is the road to Cobbs Hill Reservoir (unnamed street). Turn right and drive up the hill to the reservoir. Park on the side nearest the radio tower and look for the Washington Grove sign. GPS: N43 08.373' / W77 33.818'

The Hike

Is there no limit to the gifts George Eastman gave to Rochester? When the city approached Eastman in 1908 to fund construction of a reservoir at the top of Cobbs Hill, Eastman consented with a condition: The city must preserve the hun-

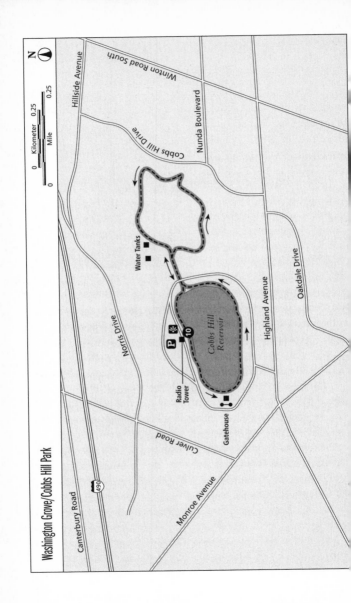

Washington Grove/Cobbs Hill Park

dred acres of mature woods adjacent to the building site. The city agreed, and this forested haven has drawn neighbors, dog walkers, and bird lovers to its heights ever since.

The crisscrossing network of trails through this hilltop woods are more confusing than the park's size might imply. With no trail names or blazes to help sort out a route, it's easy for first-time hikers to lose track of basic landmarks among the oaks and maples. We've devised a route to help you enjoy an energetic hike and find your way to the key spots in the grove and around the reservoir.

You'll begin at the radio tower on the north side of the reservoir, but descend quickly into the woods. After a circular tour of the woods, you'll ascend the short but steep hill to the top (an elevation of 636 feet), where you'll return to Cobbs Hill Reservoir, the largest water storage basin in Rochester, with a capacity of 144 million gallons. Several landmarks come into view as you circle the reservoir: first, a communications station run by Monroe County, a key element in the area's public safety system; second, the best and most photographed view in town of the Rochester city skyline; and the reservoir gatehouse, an impressive classical structure fronted by a long staircase that leads down the hillside.

Washington Grove becomes a birders' paradise in May, when passerines touch down on high ground in the middle of the night and fill the trees as they feed in the morning. Virtually every warbler, vireo, and thrush species that makes Rochester a spring stopover can be found up here, including the annual appearance of a single worm-eating warbler, flocks of chattering Tennessee warblers, and dependable sightings of gray-cheeked and Swainson's thrush. Watch the Rochester Birding Association Web site at www.rochester birding.com for guided birding walks here in mid-May.

Miles and Directions

0.0 Park near the radio tower at the top of the hill. From here, locate the Washington Grove sign and walk down the short, fairly steep hill into the woods.

0.1 At the bottom of the hill, you'll see several connecting trails. Follow the path to the right. In about 200 feet, another connecting path goes off to your left here. Continue straight.

0.2 Here's another connecting path going off to your left; keep going straight. You'll come upon another side trail in about 300 feet; just keep going straight.

0.3 Another path crosses here; continue straight along this trail.

0.5 Pass the steps that lead down to Nunda Boulevard, and continue straight along this path.

0.7 The trail bends left and leads to the blue holding tanks for the city's reservoir. When you reach the tanks (in about 450 feet), stop to acknowledge the unusually exuberant graffiti encircling the tanks. Turn left and continue on the trail.

0.9 The trail forks left and right here. Take the right trail and go up the hill to Cobbs Hill Reservoir.

1.2 Emerge from the woods on the mowed lawn surrounding the reservoir. Cross the lawn and the road, and walk up the short embankment to the paved path around the reservoir. Turn right and begin to follow the path around.

1.3 Stand here and face north, and see the best view of downtown Rochester you'll find anywhere. When you're ready, continue around the reservoir loop.

1.6 The building here is the gatehouse for Cobbs Hill Reservoir. You can see a hill with radio towers in front of you—this is Pinnacle Hill, the "other" hill in the city of Rochester, topping out at 750 feet. Continue around the loop when you're ready.

2.1 Complete your walk around the reservoir to where you began, at the parking area.

11 Genesee Valley Greenway Trail: Morgan Road to Ballantyne Road

A repurposed abandoned canal and railway corridor, the Greenway has become one of upstate New York's prettiest and most frequented trails. This tree-lined section provides a lovely hike along farmers' fields and a nature preserve.

Distance: 8.2-mile out-and-back
Approximate hiking time: 3 hours
Difficulty: Moderate (because of length)
Trail surface: Mowed path
Best season: Spring and fall; great for cross-country skiing in winter
Other trail users: Bicycles, horseback riders, snowmobiles, cross-country skiers
Canine compatibility: Dogs permitted on leash
Fees and permits: None

Schedule: Open daily dawn to dusk
Maps: National Geographic Topo! New York & New Jersey
Water availability: None
Trail contact: Friends of Genesee Valley Greenway, P.O. Box 42, Mt. Morris, NY 14510; (585) 658-2569; www.fogvg.org
Special considerations: 1. Pairs or groups of hikers often use the shuttle system on this trail, parking a car at either end rather than doubling back on the entire trail. 2. Trail can be very muddy in transitional seasons.

Finding the trailhead: From Interstate 390 North or South, take the Scottsville Road (Highway 383) exit. Turn south on Highway 383 and continue south for about 9 miles to Morgan Road. Turn right onto Morgan Road. The trailhead will come into view on your right (look for the yellow gates). Park on the side of the road, near the trailhead. GPS: N43 03.020' / W77 43.704'

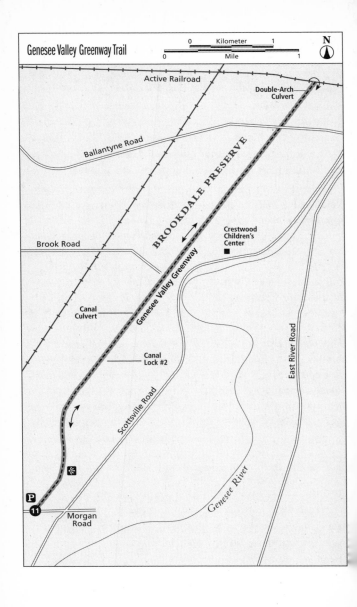

Genesee Valley Greenway Trail

0   Kilometer   1

0   Mile   1

N

Active Railroad

Double-Arch Culvert

Ballantyne Road

BROOKDALE PRESERVE

Genesee Valley Greenway

Crestwood Children's Center

Brook Road

Canal Culvert

East River Road

Canal Lock #2

Scottsville Road

Genesee River

P

11

Morgan Road

The Hike

Rochester area residents have a passion for saving abandoned railroad beds, and nowhere is their fine work more in evidence than here on the Greenway Trail. A long-distance trail that begins north of Genesee Valley Park and extends 90 miles—all the way to Hinsdale, New York—the Greenway follows the path of the Genesee Valley Canal and the Rochester branch of the Pennsylvania Railroad, turning land that had fallen into disuse into an open recreational corridor. Today, a total of about 55 miles have been completed.

Our walk begins at Morgan Road, at the south end of a particularly pleasing trail segment that passes through privately owned farmland and the Brookdale Preserve, a protected property of the Genesee Land Trust.

About 1.3 miles up the trail between Morgan and Brook Roads, you'll see a fine example of a stone lock, an exceptionally well-preserved artifact from the Genesee Valley Canal. Built in the late 1830s, this canal formed a connecting route from the Erie Canal down into New York State's southern tier, expanding the transportation of goods and materials into rural areas. This hammer-dressed cut stone lock represents the excellent workmanship with which all ninety-seven canal locks were to be constructed, but government budget cuts forced builders to substitute materials that decayed after the canal's closure. Stop here to see the technical drawings of various lock construction techniques.

The land surrounding this trail section produces a remarkable display of wildflowers in spring, and blue-winged warblers, eastern bluebirds, and field sparrows have been recorded as area breeders.

Cross Brook Road and continue into the "tunnel of green," the thick forest canopy that shelters this trail section. To your left, the Brookdale Preserve's wooded wetland can be filled with birds in spring and summer, and spring peepers begin to sing here with the first warm evenings in March. Amphibian lovers will find at least six species of frogs here: Spring peepers, western chorus, wood, northern leopard, tree, and green frogs have all been recorded on warm spring and summer evenings. The wooded areas on the right side of the trail are privately owned but no less loaded with resident birds and other creatures.

When you reach Ballantyne Road, cross here and continue north on the trail for another 0.4 mile to see one of the largest canal culverts in New York State. This double-arched culvert (under the trail) was constructed to redirect Black Creek under the Genesee Valley Canal. From here, your route north ends at the active CSX Railroad tracks. The Friends of the Genesee Valley Greenway are exploring options for creating some kind of trail passage over or around these tracks, but for now, we will use this as a turnaround point and begin walking south to return to Morgan Road.

Miles and Directions

0.0 Park along the side of the road and begin your walk at the Morgan Road entrance to the trail—look for the yellow gates and the Genesee Valley Greenway logo sign. Walk north on the trail. The Genesee Valley Canal flows to your left; you'll follow it for most of this route.

0.2 This is a great open spot from which to view the farm fields to your right. The clearing is a right-of-way for high-tension wires and a gas pipeline, creating an unobstructed viewpoint.

0.3 A small trail goes left over the canal. Continue straight.

0.9 A private road crosses the trail here. Continue straight.

1.2 Another private farm road crosses the trail to the left and right. Continue straight.

1.3 To your left is Genesee Valley Canal Lock #2. When you're ready, continue straight ahead up the trail. Soon you'll see the fences and corrals of a horse farm on the right.

1.6 A culvert below the trail allows the canal water to flow under the trail to the other side.

2.0 You've reached Brook Road. Cross the road; the trail continues on the other side. There's a parking lot to your left on the north side of Brook Road.

2.3 A trail crosses here to the left, into the Brookdale Preserve. Continue straight. The building and grounds on the right belong to Crestwood Children's Center, a support organization for children with behavioral and development issues.

2.6 Another gas pipeline right-of-way crosses the trail here. Continue straight.

2.9 Here's another old trail crossing. There's a bridge here that leads into Brookdale Preserve, but there are no official trails in the preserve to date. Continue straight.

3.5 You've reached Ballantyne Road. When traffic permits, cross the road and continue up the trail, directly to the north.

3.9 Here—under the trail—is one of the largest double culverts constructed in the nineteenth century. Built to allow Black Creek to flow under the canal, this structure is supported by wooden piles, driven down 25 feet to defeat the quicksand that surrounds the culvert.

4.1 You've reached the railroad tracks, and the end of this trail segment. Turn around and head south on the trail to return to your vehicle.

8.2 Arrive at the trailhead at Morgan Road.

12 Black Creek Park: Ridge and Wetland Trails Loop

Bring your cross-country skis and glide over this wide, mostly level loop trail through a hardwood swamp, open fields, and a compact forest of fragrant conifers. When the snow melts, this trail provides an enchanting wildlife walk.

Distance: 3.5-mile loop

Approximate hiking time: 1.5 hours

Difficulty: Easy

Trail surface: Mowed path

Best season: Spring and fall; great for cross-country skiing in winter

Other trail users: Cross-country skiers, horseback riders

Canine compatibility: Dogs permitted on leash

Fees and permits: None

Schedule: Open 7:00 a.m. to 11:00 p.m. daily

Maps: National Geographic Topo! New York & New Jersey

Water availability: Restrooms between Woodside and Pathfinder pavilions at park's Union Street entrance

Trail contact: Monroe County Parks, 171 Reservoir Avenue, Rochester 14620; (585) 753-7275; www.monroecounty.gov/parks

Finding the trailhead: From Interstate 490 on the west side of Rochester, take exit 4: Union Street/Highway 259. Turn south (left from the city, right from the western suburbs) onto Union Street/Highway 259 and continue about a mile to the park entrance on the right. GPS: N43 04.853' / W77 47.965'

The Hike

Not much development has taken place in Black Creek Park, and we can only hope that not much is planned. This generally untouched natural land makes for uncommonly

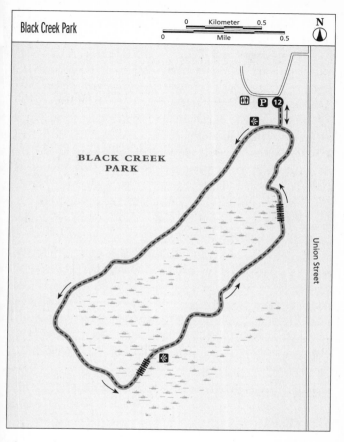

Kilometer 0 0.5
Mile 0 0.5

N

BLACK CREEK
PARK

Union Street

pleasant hiking on wide, well-maintained trails, resplendent with blooming shrubs in spring and dotted with bluebird boxes for potential spring, summer, and fall birding.

Honeysuckle, hawthorn, and autumn olive line the trail at the outset, giving way to woodland with upstate New York's characteristic oak, maple, and hickory trees that provide such a gorgeous fall display. Green's Nursery once owned land in this park, so you may see trees of unusual varieties, especially at about 1.3 miles down the trail (where the yellow arrows begin).

As you round the bend at the southern end of the trail and begin your walk back through the hardwood wetland, the trees increase in variety and wildflowers become abundant, especially in spring. In addition to the ubiquitous mayapple and marsh marigolds, look for wild geraniums, sensitive fern, and woodbine—and watch for butterflies along the sides of the path as they land on nodding flowers to feed. The mixed hardwoods include maple and ash in the wettest parts of the park, but as the path begins a steady incline beyond the wetland and the water levels recede, you'll find black walnut, hickory, and staghorn sumac, as well as beech and spruce.

It's easy to see deer tracks in the wetter areas, and it's very likely you'll spot a deer darting through the trees or even crossing your path. Watch for wild turkey, a frequent feeder along this trail, as well as eastern cottontail, red fox, and the ever-present gray squirrel and eastern chipmunk. Songbirds—including warblers—frequent the southernmost portion of the trail before the first boardwalk in the wooded areas, but you are likely to see cardinals, chickadees, goldfinches, and other common species just about anywhere along the route.

Miles and Directions

0.0   The trail begins at the parking lot off Union Street. Follow the trailhead signs.

0.2   Turn right to follow the maroon arrows. Note that the plastic directional arrows are fairly worn and bleached by sun and weather, so colors may not be readily apparent.

0.3   The observation point on the right side of the trail looks down into a clearing and beyond to the woods. This sledding hill becomes very popular in winter.

0.4 A cross trail here provides access to the picnic pavilions. Continue straight. You're walking through an area of low foliage and shrubs.

0.8 A trail with blue blazes goes right here. Continue straight.

1.1 Here the trail moves into a wooded area, with plenty of shade and taller trees.

1.3 A blue-blazed trail goes right here; continue straight. In a moment, the maroon arrows continue straight here to another parking area. Turn left and begin following the yellow arrows.

1.5 A side trail goes right; follow the yellow arrow straight ahead. Here a slight incline begins as you leave the woods and cross more open land.

1.6 A blue trail goes right here. Continue to the left as the blue trail goes straight ahead of you.

1.8 A wooden boardwalk provides dry passage over the hardwood swamp.

2.0 You've reached a high point in the trail, where it's easy to view some of the slightly lower areas in the woods. A bench to your right provides a resting place while you pause to enjoy the wooded land.

2.3 As you round this bend, a side trail to the right goes to Mill Creek. Continue to the left.

2.7 From here, a side trail provides access to Union Street. Continue to follow the yellow arrows to the left.

2.8 Here is another boardwalk over swampland. Just after the bridge, you'll enter a dense conifer forest, which extends for about 0.1 mile.

3.0 A blue-blazed trail goes off to the left here; continue straight and enter an area of shrubs and lower foliage.

3.2 A side trail takes a shortcut to Union Street. Continue straight.

3.3 Turn right here to return to the parking lot.

3.5 Arrive back at the beginning of your hike.

13 Lehigh Valley Trail: Rush Hamlet to Rochester Junction

This segment of the 15-mile Rails-to-Trails project follows the meandering Honeoye Creek through woodland and family farms, ending at a perfect picnic spot in Mendon.

Distance: 2.6-mile shuttle, or 5.2-mile out-and-back

Approximate hiking time: 1.5 to 2.5 hours

Difficulty: Easy

Trail surface: Compacted cinder trail

Best season: May and June, September through November

Other trail users: Bicycles, joggers, cross-country skiers, horseback riders

Canine compatibility: Dogs permitted on leash

Fees and permits: None

Schedule: Open daily dawn to dusk

Maps: National Geographic Topo! New York & New Jersey

Water availability: Water, restrooms, and snacks available in Rush on Highway 15A

Trail contact: Monroe County Parks, 171 Reservoir Avenue, Rochester 14620; (585) 753-7275; www.monroecounty.gov/parks

Special considerations: This section of trail is open to snowmobiles.

Finding the trailhead: From Interstate 390 South, take the Rush exit (11). Turn right at the end of the ramp. Drive to Highway 15A and turn left. Cross Highway 251 and watch for Rush Veterans Memorial Park on your left. Pass the park; a sign on your left immediately after the park reads LEHIGH VALLEY TRAIL. Turn left and park on the roadside at the trailhead.

To reach the Rochester Junction trailhead on Plains Road in Mendon, take Highway 65 (Clover Street) from Rochester and drive south to Mendon. Turn right onto Highway 251 and continue to

Lehigh Valley Trail: Rush Hamlet to Rochester Junction

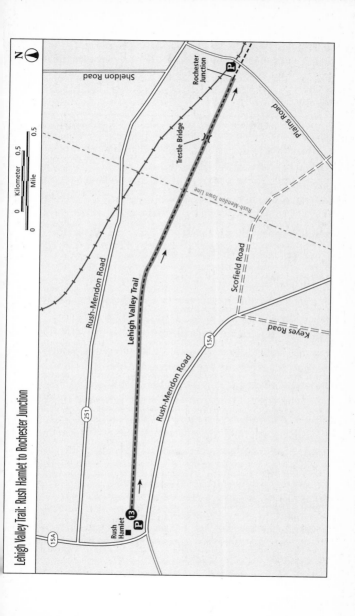

N

0 Kilometer 0.5
0 Mile 0.5

Sheldon Road

Rochester Junction

Trestle Bridge

Plains Road

Rush-Mendon Town Line

Rush-Mendon Road

Scofield Road

Keyes Road

Lehigh Valley Trail

Rush-Mendon Road

251

15A

15A

Rush Hamlet

13

Plains Road. Turn left onto Plains and continue to the park at Rochester Junction. The parking lot for the trail is on the right. GPS: N43 59.523' / W77 35.088'

The Hike

It's estimated that half a million trains passed through this corridor when the Lehigh Valley Railroad ran anthracite—coal that burned so cleanly, it was nicknamed "black diamond"—from mining sites in Pennsylvania to Buffalo for transport west. From 1892 through the 1950s, this route provided scenic passage for travelers as well as coal, covering 435 miles from New York City to Buffalo and passing through Victor, Mendon, and Rush, with junctions in Henrietta and Rochester.

When the heyday of railroads as the nation's principal freight haulers had faded, the tracks remained—and in 1976, when this corridor was fated for obscurity, Monroe County acquired the land for its future use. In 2004 the 15-mile Lehigh Valley Trail became a connecting long-distance walkway and bikeway between the Auburn Trail to the east and the Genesee Valley Greenway Trail to the west.

From Rush Hamlet to Rochester Junction, this uncommonly pleasant trail segment offers an excellent surface for hiking, biking, and horseback riding, with a sheltering canopy of foliage that provides welcome shade along the 2.6-mile route.

Miles and Directions

0.0 Enter the trail at Rush Hamlet, and walk east toward Mendon. You'll see green half-mile markers on the trail as you walk.

0.7 An unmarked trail goes left here. Continue straight.

1.8 A sign here indicates the Rush-Mendon town line. From here, you're walking in the town of Mendon.

2.1 Cross the trestle bridge here and continue east.

2.6 You've reached Rochester Junction, and the end of this segment of the trail. For a longer hike, cross the street and continue to follow the trail, which extends for another 8 miles to the east.

14 Mendon Ponds Park: Birdsong and Quaker Pond Trails

This very popular hike offers a multitude of pleasures: the opportunity to feed birds by hand, a well-interpreted trail with informative kiosks that help with flora and fauna identification, and an extended walk through a glacially sculpted landscape.

Distance: 4.8-mile loop
Approximate hiking time: 2.5 hours
Difficulty: Moderate
Trail surface: Wide dirt path
Best season: April through June, September through November; also a great winter hike
Other trail users: None
Canine compatibility: Dogs not permitted
Fees and permits: None
Schedule: Open daily dawn to dusk

Maps: National Geographic Topo! New York & New Jersey
Water availability: At Nature Center, where trail begins
Trail contact: Monroe County Parks, 171 Reservoir Avenue, Rochester 14620; (585) 753-7275; www.monroecounty.gov/parks
Special considerations: In winter and early spring, bring black oil sunflower seeds to hand-feed birds and squirrels. In summer, bug repellent is a must. Poison ivy and poison sumac both grow here.

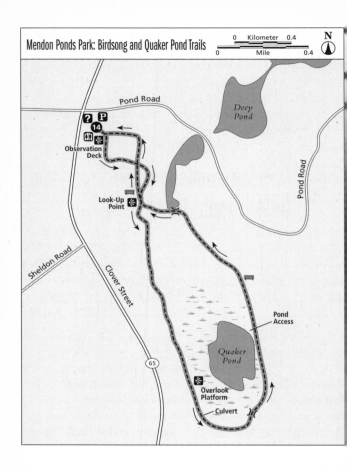

Mendon Ponds Park: Birdsong and Quaker Pond Trails

Pond Road

Deep Pond

Pond Road

Observation Deck

Look-Up Point

Sheldon Road

Clover Street

65

Pond Access

Quaker Pond

Overlook Platform

Culvert

0   Kilometer   0.4
0   Mile   0.4

N

Finding the trailhead: From Interstate 590 South in Rochester, take exit 2B for Highway 31/Monroe Avenue. Merge onto Monroe Avenue at the end of the ramp, and in 0.3 mile, turn right onto Clover Street. Drive about 7 miles on Clover to the third park entrance, on Pond Road (look for the Nature Center sign). Turn left into the park and take the first right into the Nature Center parking lot. GPS: N43 01.348' / W77 35.088'

The Hike

A product of the Wisconsin ice sheet that covered upstate New York some 12,000 to 14,000 years ago, Mendon Ponds Park provides some excellent examples of glacial features including kames—small, conical hills of gravel and rock, left behind as the glaciers melted. The ice melt formed lakes, but most of these lakes drained away or evaporated, leaving the kames as the only clue they had existed. You can see kame formations on the straight trail as you walk toward Quaker Pond.

On the trail's first leg, be sure you have your black oil sunflower seeds or peanut chips handy for the black-capped chickadees and their friends, especially in winter and early spring. These cheeky little birds will begin to scold you as you reach them, and when you stand very still with a handful of seed outstretched, they will land on your hand and take a single seed each, flying back into the trees to hammer the seed open and eat the contents. If you linger, especially in winter, red-breasted nuthatches and tufted titmice may join in the feasting. Gray and red squirrels, also eager for treats, may actually sit up and beg for you. (A particularly bold gray squirrel actually climbed up onto my shoe and stood on my foot to get my attention.)

Bayberry, alders, and red maple are just some of the trees that line the trail here, and wildflowers are plentiful along the trail's edges and on the forest floor. Here you can choose a shorter walk and turn back on Birdsong Trail rather than continuing out to Quaker Pond, enjoying the interpretive displays along the shorter trail.

The birds' food-begging behavior continues as you leave Birdsong Trail and begin your loop around Quaker

Pond, a serene pool in the midst of a wider wetland area. Muskrats frequently swim across the pond in full view, and mink, weasels, opossum, and red and gray foxes make use of the area. Flying squirrels have been spotted here in early morning and at dusk. Painted, spotted, and snapping turtles, salamanders, spring peepers, and several other frogs are often seen here.

Watch for evidence of beavers as you scan the pond from several different overlooks, as these industrious creatures have made this pond their home for decades. All kinds of wetland plants thrive here, including several species of loosestrife, willows, cottonwoods, gray dogwood, alder thickets, viburnum, and highbush cranberry.

Miles and Directions

0.0 The trail begins at the Nature Center parking lot. Follow the signs for Old Orchard Trail and Birdsong Trail. Turn left at the wide path at the edge of the meadow, and stop at the observation deck to the right to view the meadow and spot wildlife. From here, Old Orchard Trail leads to Birdsong Trail.

0.1 Turn right onto Birdsong Trail. There's a kiosk here with information about the park's soil content and geological origins.

0.4 The trail forks here. The left trail goes back to the Nature Center and parking lot. Take the right trail.

0.5 From here, you'll see a purple blaze with a white outline. This is the blaze for Quaker Pond Trail. Turn right onto this trail and continue uphill.

0.7 Here you come to Look-Up Point, a gathering place for outdoor nature programs. Bear right up the trail.

0.8 The trail to your right goes back to the Nature Center. Continue straight.

2.2 A little-used bridle path to Clover Street goes right from here. Continue straight.

2.6 Look for the tree with the double trunk to the left of the trail. There's a dirt path here to an overlook platform, with a great view of Quaker Pond.

2.8 Another bridle path goes to the right; continue straight. In about 350 feet, you'll come to a culvert that allows a stream to pass under the trail.

3.0 A connector trail to the Southern Meadow Loop Trail goes right here, while Quaker Pond goes left. Turn left and continue to follow the purple blazes.

3.1 This bridge crosses Quaker Pond, providing a wonderful place to scan for birds along the pond's reedy edges or watch for muskrats, turtles, and other pond creatures.

3.3 In about 250 feet, the trail splits three ways; continue to follow the purple blazes to the left.

3.7 A short trail to the left provides access to the pond.

3.9 Quaker Pond Trail continues straight; two other trails go off to the northeast and southeast. Go straight. In about 500 feet, Lookout Trail goes off to the right. Continue on Quaker Pond Trail.

4.0 You'll cross Lookout Trail again. Keep going straight.

4.3 Here the Quaker Pond and Swamp Trails meet for the return leg of each. Follow the purple blazes straight, and stop in about 400 feet to see a different view of Quaker Pond from the bridge. At the next intersection, continue straight.

4.4 Turn right here to return to the Nature Center.

4.8 You've reached the Nature Center and the end of your hike; the parking lot is to your right.

15 Powder Mills Park: Trillium and Ridge Trails

One of the area's most popular hiking and cross-country skiing trails, this loop offers an easy amble along a marsh and a stimulating ascent to a sweeping view of western Monroe County.

Distance: 1.3-mile loop
Approximate hiking time: 45 minutes
Difficulty: Moderate
Trail surface: Dirt path
Best season: May and June, September through November, snowy winter days
Other trail users: Cross-country skiers
Canine compatibility: Dogs permitted on leash
Fees and permits: None
Schedule: Open daily 7:00 a.m. to 11:00 p.m., closing at 4:00 p.m. in winter.
Maps: National Geographic Topo! New York & New Jersey
Water availability: Water and restrooms available near the parking lot as you enter the East Area picnic grounds from Park Road
Trail contact: Monroe County Parks, 171 Reservoir Avenue, Rochester 14620; (585) 753-7275; www.monroecounty.gov/parks

Finding the trailhead: From Interstate 490 East, take exit 28 for Highway 96. Turn right onto Highway 96 at the end of the exit ramp. Drive 0.5 mile to the park entrance. Turn right onto Park Road. Pass Corduroy Road and the fish hatchery on your left, and continue on Park Road to the next left. Turn here and drive to the end of the road at Wadhams pavilion. The trailhead is behind the pavilion. GPS: N43 02.740' / W77 28.877'

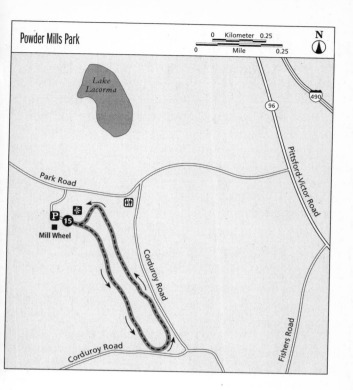

The Hike

Before you begin this hike, you'll see a wooden mill wheel standing on a narrow spot in Irondequoit Creek, just in front of the Wadhams pavilion. The location is no accident: Powder Mills Park gets its name from the Rand-Wadhams Mill, which operated here from 1850 until 1910. Its product was blasting powder, an inexpensive gunpowder made from saltpeter, sulfur, and charcoal—and the waterpower afforded by the rushing creek made this a perfect spot to grind these essentials into the requisite fine powder. When business fell off with the advent of new explosive materials, the mill closed down and its buildings fell into disrepair. Monroe County stepped in and turned this area into a public park in 1929, making it one of the area's most frequented natural spaces.

The attraction comes, in part, from the abundance of varied habitats compacted into a fairly small area. On this hike, you'll trace the line between Irondequoit Creek's watershed marsh and a glacier-created ridge, passing first along the wetland with wildflowers, scouring rushes, alder and witch hazel shrubs to your right and the wooded hillside to your left—a sight to see in fall, when the maple, beech, basswood, sassafras, and American hornbeam turn brilliant shades of crimson and ginger.

The two trails involved in this hike do not connect officially, but it's simple to follow the trail around the hillside at its south end to continue on the hill's east flank. Once you've made this turn, the trail begins to climb up onto the ridge, culminating in a viewpoint (with a bench) from which you can enjoy a terrific vista of western Monroe County.

Miles and Directions

0.0   Enter the trail behind Wadhams pavilion. In about 200 feet, the trail divides into the Yellow and Blue Trails. Take the Yellow Trail, straight ahead. This is the Trillium Trail.

0.3   You're walking along the wetland that flanks Irondequoit Creek to your right. To the left, one of Powder Mills Park's characteristic hills rises about 80 feet. A cross-country ski trail goes right here. Continue straight.

0.5 A cross-country ski trail marked "easiest" goes right from here. Continue straight into the parking lot, and bear left around the bottom of the hill. The blazes end here as you cross over from the Trillium Trail to continue on the Ridge Trail (Blue Trail). In about 250 feet, you'll come to Corduroy Road. Walk along the road for about 100 feet until you see the trail on your left.

0.6 Follow the blue blazes up the hill. In about 250 feet, an unblazed trail will appear on your left. Continue straight. From here, a steady incline leads to the ridge.

0.7 The incline ends at the top of the ridge. From here, it's a fairly level walk to the ridge overlook.

0.9 You've reached a confusing intersection of three trails. If you'd like to make the short, upward climb to the ridge overlook, take the rightmost of the three trails on your left (the one that leads uphill). If you'd prefer to head back to the trailhead, take the trail farthest to the left. If you take the short walk to the ridge, there's a bench here at the top where you can stop and admire the view of western Monroe County from your lofty elevation of 500 feet. When you're ready, turn and take the path down the wood-reinforced stairs to start back to the trailhead. Do not try to climb straight down from the ridge—the park discourages this dangerous route.

1.1 Turn right here onto the White Trail and walk downhill. In about 325 feet, turn right onto the Yellow Trail.

1.3 Arrive back at the trailhead.

16 Thousand Acre Swamp

Actually about 500 acres, this Nature Conservancy holding is one of the largest remaining wetlands in Monroe County. Stroll through a swamp on a raised boardwalk, cross a marshy lowland woods and a hardwood forest, and skirt the edge of a wild meadow before coming to the preserve's hidden pond.

Distance: 2.6-mile lollipop
Approximate hiking time: 1.5 hours
Difficulty: Easy
Trail surface: Mixed: mowed tracks, dirt path, and boardwalk
Best season: May and June, September through November
Other trail users: None
Canine compatibility: Dogs not permitted
Fees and permits: None
Schedule: Open daily dawn to dusk
Maps: National Geographic Topo! New York & New Jersey
Water availability: None
Trail contact: The Nature Conservancy, 1048 University Avenue; Rochester 14607 (585) 546-8030; www.nature.org
Special considerations: Wear insect repellent May through August. Some muddy spots in spring; remain on trails to avoid poison ivy.

Finding the trailhead: From Interstate 590 North, take the Browncroft Boulevard/Highway 286 exit. Turn right (east) at the end of the ramp. Drive 4.9 miles (Browncroft will become Atlantic Avenue; continue straight) to Jackson Road. Turn left onto Jackson and continue 0.5 mile until you are just past the Penfield Volunteer ambulance station. Watch for the wooden Thousand Acre Swamp sign on your left, and turn left onto the dirt road. Take the road to the end (you'll pass a private driveway on your right—keep going). The parking lot and trailhead are at the end of the dirt road. The road and parking lot are not plowed in winter. GPS: N43 10.040' / W77 27.069'

The Hike

Take the Entrance Trail to Deer Run, passing trailheads for the smaller Songbird Trail, Trillium Trail, and Weasel Way. At the end of Deer Run, turn right onto the 610-foot boardwalk through the most saturated part of this wetland. Here lie the headwaters of both Hipp Brook and Four Mile Creek, two waterways that flow several miles north to Irondequoit Bay.

At the end of the boardwalk, enter the wooded marshland on the Warbler Fen Trail. Warbler Fen becomes Hermit Walk, extending to the east toward the Meadow. Stop here to notice the 8-foot-high exposed root systems of several fallen trees—casualties, perhaps, of the ice storms that lay heavy, frozen coats over the county in late winter. Hermit Walk can be a great place to spot animals and their young: White-tailed deer, raccoons, chipmunks, eastern cottontails, red foxes, and even coyotes live and breed here.

After a small creek, the trail inclines gently, enough to create a dry area where silver maples, oaks, and tulip trees thrive. Spring songbirds can include scarlet tanager; rose-breasted grosbeak; black-and-white, Blackburnian, and Nashville warblers; American redstart; white-eyed vireo; and northern mockingbird.

Hermit Walk ends at the Meadow. In spring and summer, stop here and look across to check the eastern bluebird boxes placed here by The Nature Conservancy. The meadow grasses remain tall until late summer, sustaining a season-long riot of black-eyed Susans, Canada goldenrod, and other brightly colored wildflowers.

You reach another wet woodland at the end of the Meadows Trail on the path to Way Pond. Walk around the

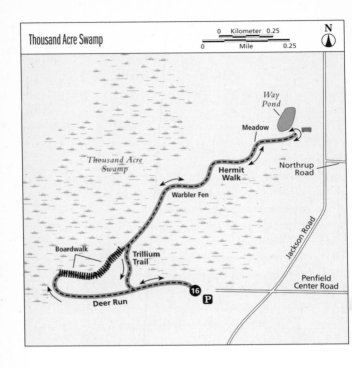

edge of the pond to the other side, where a bench provides an excellent view of the small, weedy island in the middle of the pond. In early spring, you may spot a Canada goose sitting on a nest on the island; later in the season, catch glimpses of goslings or ducklings learning to swim.

You'll retrace your route from Way Pond to return to Hermit Walk and Trillium Trail, which crosses the woods toward the parking lot. At the end of Trillium Trail, you'll reach Deer Run. Turn left here and continue to the parking lot.

Miles and Directions

0.0 The Entrance Trail begins at the parking lot. Stop here at the kiosk to check bird and animal sightings recorded by recent visitors.

0.2 Trillium Trail begins to the right; continue straight on Deer Run. In summer, watch for adult and young animals along this trail.

0.3 Weasel Way begins to the right; continue straight on Deer Run.

0.4 The boardwalk begins; turn right and cross the wettest part of the swamp. Look for robins nesting in trees close to the boardwalk, and for herons and ducks hidden between the cattails. There's a bench and viewing area halfway along the boardwalk.

0.6 Continue straight on Warbler Fen/Hermit Walk to the Meadow. Look for interesting mosses and lichens on tree trunks close to the ground.

1.2 Take the Meadows Trail to the right and cross two grassy meadows filled with wildflowers in spring and summer.

1.5 You've arrived at Way Pond and the end of the trail. Continue to the bench on the south side of the pond, and look for nesting geese and ducks or green frogs and painted turtles. When you're ready, turn around and retrace your steps along the Way Pond Trail, back across the Meadows Trail and into the woods at Hermit Walk. Continue back through the hardwood forest and into the lower wetland until you reach Trillium Trail, which goes off to your left.

2.2 Turn left onto Trillium Trail. Cross the forest on this trail for less than 0.25 mile.

2.4 Turn left and walk 0.2 mile to return to the parking lot.

2.6 Arrive back at the parking lot.

17 Erie Canal Heritage Trail: Pittsford to Fairport

This historic canal towpath is now an 84–mile recreational trail, a developed stretch of the canal's total 360 miles. This section reveals the canal's famous Great Embankment, meanders through three charming towns, and offers food, drink, and services at each end and at its midpoint.

Distance: 6-mile one-way shuttle
Approximate hiking time: 3 hours
Difficulty: Moderate
Trail surface: Some paved, mostly crushed stone
Best season: April through November
Other trail users: Bicycles, in-line skaters in paved areas, cross-country skiers
Canine compatibility: Dogs permitted on leash
Fees and permits: None

Schedule: Open daily dawn to dusk
Maps: National Geographic Topo! New York & New Jersey
Water availability: In Pittsford's Schoen Place at the outset, in Bushnell's Basin at the midpoint, and in the village of Fairport at the end
Trail contact: New York State Canal Corporation, 200 Southern Boulevard, Albany 12201; (518) 436-2700; www.nyscanals.gov

Finding the trailhead: From Interstate 590 North or South, take the Monroe Avenue/Pittsford exit and turn east onto Monroe Avenue (Highway 31). Drive 2.5 miles through Brighton and Pittsford to the village of Pittsford. Turn left onto Highway 96 (North Main Street), cross the Erie Canal, and take the next right on Schoen Place. Drive through Schoen Place to Bill Wahl's Ice Cream & Yogurt Parlor on your left and turn after the building, driving down the slope into the parking lot. We'll begin the hike at the gazebo across the road from Bill Wahl's, alongside the canal.

In Fairport, take Interstate 490 east to the Fairport/Highway 31F exit (25). Turn left at the end of the ramp and drive 2.5 miles to O'Connor Road. Turn left and drive to the second parking lot. The canal path is in front of you, along the north side of the canal. GPS: N43 05.398' / W77 30.669'

The Hike

We won't actually travel "15 miles on the Erie Canal"— we'll stop at 6, enough for a satisfying walk along the water on a fine spring day or a crisp fall afternoon. In the canal's heyday, mules did indeed walk this towpath to propel barges up and down the water's length, and you'll gain some appreciation for their labors as you stride along this historic, enduringly appealing pathway.

A little canal history: This is the waterway that transformed the way business was done throughout New York State, transporting goods and materials that came up the Hudson River from New York City into upstate New York, across the state and on to Lake Erie, where these shipments could reach into the western frontier. With merchandise traveling at many times the speed of a horse and wagon, settlements to the west could grow and prosper, opening new territories to construction and enterprise.

Today, this peaceful canal transports little more than pleasure crafts and tour boats, but its place in history is sealed— and thanks to the foresight of organizations including the New York State Canal Corporation and the Erie Canalway National Heritage Corridor, the Erie Canal Heritage Trail is one of the most popular pathways from Albany to Buffalo.

You'll pass through three canal town centers on this hike: Pittsford, Bushnell's Basin (actually a hamlet of Perinton), and Fairport, while walking straight across Perinton

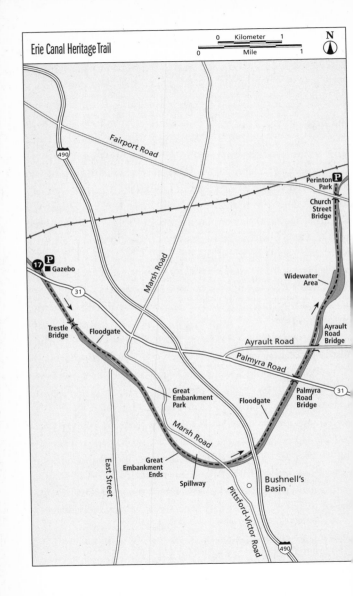

Erie Canal Heritage Trail

0 — Kilometer — 1
0 — Mile — 1

N

Fairport Road

490

Perinton Park P

Church Street Bridge

Widewater Area

17 P ■ Gazebo

31

Marsh Road

Trestle Bridge

Floodgate

Ayrault Road

Palmyra Road

Ayrault Road Bridge

Palmyra Road Bridge

31

Great Embankment Park

Floodgate

Marsh Road

East Street

Great Embankment Ends

Spillway

Bushnell's Basin

Pittsford-Victor Road

490

to reach Fairport from Pittsford. All three of these towns offer shopping and dining experiences right on the canal, from the boutiques and gift emporia of Schoen Place to the quirky shops in Fairport's Packett's Landing.

And here's the most important note of all: In each town, you'll find one of Rochester's premier ice cream establishments, all of which make their own confections. In Pittsford, your hike begins in front of Bill Wahl's Ice Cream & Yogurt Parlor, where ice cream is made right on the premises. Bushnell's Basin features the world-famous Abbott's Frozen Custard—a creamier concoction than ice cream—and they've been perfecting their astonishing chocolate almond custard since 1902, so be sure to stop for a taste. In Fairport, the Moonlight Creamery offers all-natural artisan ice cream in rich flavors like Second Date, Inauguration Day, and Maui Wowie, along with shade-grown coffee and handmade chocolates. After walking 6 miles, you'll deserve a treat!

Miles and Directions

0.0 Begin the hike at the gazebo in front of Bill Wahl's Ice Cream & Yogurt Parlor. Walk east (to your left as you face the canal) under the trestle bridge.

0.6 A trestle bridge for Highway 31 passes overhead. Continue straight along the canal.

0.9 A connector trail goes down to the left into a Pittsford neighborhood. To your right, you can see the first of two floodgates you'll pass on this hike. Floodgates are a precaution in the event that a canal wall breaks, to keep the water from flooding the surrounding neighborhood.

1.1 Another neighborhood connector trail begins here to your left. Continue straight.

1.5 You've reached Great Embankment Park. A mile long and 70 feet high, the Great Embankment was hand-constructed by men with shovels in 1822 to keep the canal from draining into the Irondequoit Creek Valley. It persists in this purpose today, and the Town of Pittsford has added a pleasant, grassy park with picnic tables and benches. This is a nice place to stop and rest.

2.1 A neighborhood connector trail goes off to the left here. Continue straight.

2.3 Here the Great Embankment ends.

2.4 Notice the water cascading down a stepped spillway to your left.

2.6 To your left, there's road access through a parking lot. If you're hiking in winter, you will certainly notice that from this point on, the Town of Perinton has cleared the snow from the trail.

2.7 The Marsh Road bridge crosses the canal overhead. You can access the bridge using a path to the left of the trail (after you pass under the bridge). Across the canal from here, the mercantile area for Bushnell's Basin, a hamlet of Perinton, offers services including Finger Lakes Coffee Roasters, Abbott's Frozen Custard, more restaurants, and restrooms at the Mobil service station.

3.0 I-490 passes overhead. Continue straight.

3.4 On your right, you'll see the second floodgate you'll pass on this walk.

3.9 Pass under the Palmyra Road bridge. If you like, you can access the road using the paths on the left, on either side of the bridge.

4.3 Ayrault Road passes overhead. You can access the road using the paths on either side of the bridge, to your left.

4.6 Wooden stairs to your left lead down into a Perinton neighborhood.

4.9 You've reached Fullam's Basin, one of the widest points in the canal. When a canal improvement project shortened and straightened the route in the mid-1800s, crews built a straight embankment across an old loop in the canal at this point, allowing the water to fill in the difference. The result was this "widewater," a favorite stop for tour boats. A stairway to your left leads to the right-of-way for the high tension wires that pass overhead. People often walk or cross-country ski through this wide swath of clear land. Continue straight on the canal path.

5.4 To the left, an access path leads into a residential neighborhood. Continue straight; you are now passing into Fairport.

5.7 Cross under the Church Street bridge. Perinton Park is straight ahead.

6.0 You have arrived in Perinton Park. If you planned a shuttle hike, you'll find your second car in the parking lot here. You may wish to walk (or drive) another 0.5 mile into the village of Fairport, where you will find services including restaurants, the Moonlight Creamery, and Fairport Coffee.

18 Corbett's Glen Nature Park

This sparkling gem on the border between Brighton and Penfield takes you on a delightful wander to Postcard Falls, a bubbling cascade on Allens Creek, secreted by the surrounding mature woods and the glen's steep hills. If you take only one hike in the Rochester area, make it this one.

Distance: 2-mile loop
Approximate hiking time: 1 hour
Difficulty: Moderate
Trail surface: Dirt path
Best season: April through November, also beautiful on bright winter days
Other trail users: Cross-country skiers
Canine compatibility: Dogs permitted on leash
Fees and permits: None
Schedule: Open daily 7:00 a.m. to 10:00 p.m.
Maps: National Geographic Topo! New York & New Jersey
Water availability: None
Trail contact: Town of Brighton Recreation and Parks Department, 220 Idlewood Road, Rochester 14618; (585) 784-5260; www.townofbrighton.org
Genesee Land Trust, 500 East Avenue, Rochester 14607; (585) 256-2130; www.genesee landtrust.org

Finding the trailhead: From Interstate 490 East, take the Penfield Road exit. Turn left at the end of the ramp and drive 0.6 mile to the Corbett's Glen Nature Park parking lot. GPS: N43 08.241' / W77 31.601'

The Hike

If you don't know about Corbett's Glen, it's not a surprise that you've missed it—this seventy-three-acre preserve is surrounded by suburban development, hidden by the steep limestone walls of Allens Creek Valley. This enchanting bit of wilderness has become a landscape cherished by neighborhood associations, including the Allens Creek/Corbett's Glen Preservation Group, who worked with the Genesee Land Trust to protect this valley from encroaching commercial interests. The result: You can walk 2 miles of uninterrupted trails here along the creek and through unspoiled woods and fields, or sit by Postcard Falls and watch the creek's waters cascade over a series of rocky ledges.

Your hike—beginning at the parking area on Penfield Road—wanders along tree-lined trails and up and down slopes of glacial moraine, now blanketed with wild ground covers and forest floor–dwelling wildflowers. Look for the area's spring favorites, including trillium and violets, as well as bittersweet, cardinal flowers, and many others. Birds are plentiful here at any time of year: Watch for Carolina wren, northern mockingbird, gray catbird, and tufted titmouse year-round, along with raptors hunting in the meadow and the occasional owl sleeping against a tree's trunk, blending in with its surroundings.

You'll hear rushing water as you approach Allens Creek, and Postcard Falls comes into view after the bend to the left. On your approach, you'll see a railroad bridge that remains from the nineteenth century, constructed using the glen's own bedrock stone. Don't miss this sight in winter, when the water sparkles off the surrounding snow and ice.

Four-footed wildlife abounds in this nature park, so be on the lookout for white-tailed deer, red fox, opossum, and even mink. You may spot anglers enjoying the creek's bounty of salmon and rainbow trout, and the creek side is a worthy place to search for frogs, salamanders, and turtles.

On your way back through the glen, you'll pass through a meadow full of billowing grasses and nodding wildflowers,

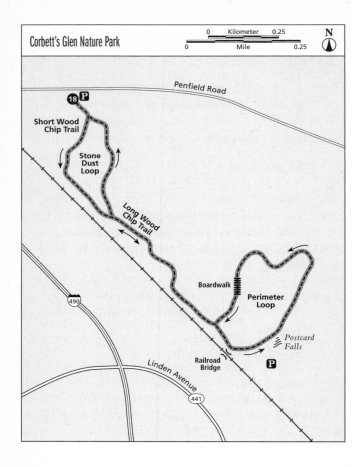

Corbett's Glen Nature Park

Kilometer

0   0.25

Mile

0   0.25

N

Penfield Road

18 P

Short Wood
Chip Trail

Stone
Dust
Loop

Long Wood
Chip Trail

490

Boardwalk

Perimeter
Loop

Postcard
Falls

Linden Avenue

Railroad
Bridge

P

441

many of which have probably grown here for centuries. Enjoy
the show from spring to late summer, and watch for grassland
birds including field and savannah sparrows, bobolinks, eastern
meadowlarks, red-winged blackbirds, and eastern bluebirds.
Wild turkeys make the glen their home as well.

Miles and Directions

0.0 Begin the hike from the parking lot. In about 250 feet, turn right onto Stone Dust Loop. (While these trails are not labeled with their names in the glen, we'll use their names for reference, as additional signs may be posted in the future.)

0.1 Follow the green blazes to the right to begin Short Wood Chip Trail. The trail goes to the left here as well; we'll take that route on our return trip.

0.3 Short Wood Chip Loop ends here; follow the red blazes onto Long Wood Chip Trail.

0.5 There's a steep downward slope here, followed in a few feet by a slope back up to your current level. If you prefer to skip this up-and-down activity, you can go around it on a path to your right.

0.6 A break in the fence to your left provides access to Park Lane in Brighton. Continue straight. In about 200 feet, Long Wood Chip Trail ends as you enter the Perimeter Trail loop. You can hear falling water from here as you approach Allens Creek and Postcard Falls. Cross the road (actually a driveway). A railroad bridge forms a tunnel here over Allens Creek, and the deck overlook in front of you provides a nice viewing point for the short waterfall. (This is not Postcard Falls; that's coming up in a moment.) A narrow pedestrian bridge to your left extends over the creek, dead-ending on the hill face across the water. Continue along the creek.

0.8 Here is Postcard Falls. For a great view and excellent photo opportunities, walk out onto the exposed creek bed in front of you and along the creek to your left.

0.9 The South Meadow Trail, to your left, crosses the open meadow here. This is a wonderful place to see wildflowers in spring and early summer. Continue straight—following the orange blazes—or shorten your walk by turning left here and crossing the meadow. If you're going straight, you'll see the

Cross Meadow Trail (blue blazes) to your left in about 200 feet. Continue straight.

1.1 The Cross Meadow Trail emerges here to your left. Continue downhill into the wetland.

1.2 A boardwalk begins here, providing a dry crossing over this marsh. If it's a spring evening, you're sure to hear peepers here. The boardwalk extends for about 300 feet, and then ends as the South Meadow Trail emerges from the open field. Continue to follow the orange blazes.

1.3 Turn right onto the Long Wood Chip Trail and begin the hike back to the beginning of the trail by following the red blazes.

1.7 Bear right and follow the green blazes around the other side of Short Wood Chip Trail.

1.9 The green blazes end here as you join the Stone Dust Loop. Follow the blue blazes to the right.

2.0 Arrive back at the trailhead at the Penfield Road parking lot.

19 Crescent Trail: Horizon Hill Conservation Area

With an elevation change of 278 feet, this is the most challenging hike described in this guide—but the view from the top makes the climb worth the effort, and the secluded, wooded hills provide a refreshing sense of wilderness in a commercially developed area.

Distance: 2.1-mile loop
Approximate hiking time: 1.5 hours
Difficulty: More challenging
Trail surface: Narrow dirt path
Best season: April through November
Other trail users: Joggers, mountain bikers (illegal, but present), cross-country skiers
Canine compatibility: Dogs permitted on leash; you will see dogs running free, but this is illegal
Fees and permits: None
Schedule: Open daily dawn to dusk

Maps: National Geographic Topo! New York & New Jersey; also Town of Perinton Web site (see Trail contact)
Water availability: Vendors in Bushnell's Basin and at Lodge at Woodcliff, at top of hill
Trail contact: Crescent Trail Association, P.O. Box 1354, Fairport 14450; (585) 234-1621; www.perinton.org/Departments .RandP/hikingctha/
Special considerations: Ice gripping footwear is strongly recommended for winter and early spring hiking.

Finding the trailhead: From Interstate 490, take the Bushnell's Basin exit (27). Turn left at the end of the ramp and drive to Garnsey Road. Turn left on Garnsey and drive to the Horizon Hill Conservation Area parking lot on the right side of the road, after the Harris Beach LLC office building. GPS: N43 03.168' / W77 27.830'

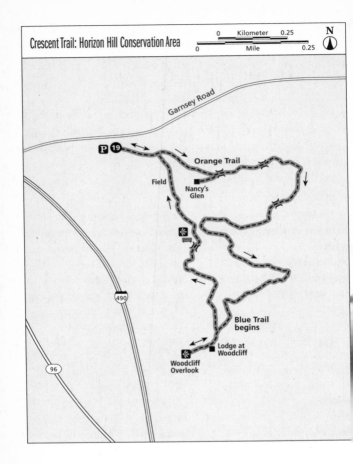

Crescent Trail: Horizon Hill Conservation Area

Kilometer 0.25
Mile 0.25

N

Garnsey Road

P 19

Orange Trail

Field

Nancy's Glen

490

Blue Trail begins

Lodge at Woodcliff

Woodcliff Overlook

96

The Hike

We can't say enough about the people of Perinton and their commitment to creating and preserving wilderness trails. The Crescent Trail, a 35-mile network of footpaths used by hikers, runners, and nature lovers, winds through parks and preserved open spaces all over town, including some private lands. The section we will explore takes you to the top of Horizon Hill, a viewpoint from which you can enjoy a sweeping panorama of Monroe and Ontario Counties to the south and west.

Begin at the Garnsey Road parking lot and follow the orange-blazed trail into the woods and up the hill. You'll follow the Orange Trail to the top of the hill and on to the Horizon Hill overlook, and then take the blue-blazed trail back to the parking lot.

In just a few feet the trail begins to climb, taking you into the glacial hills and valleys created when melting ice sheets receded across this land some 12,000 years ago, leaving huge piles of gravel and earth in their stead. Now covered by deciduous woods, these hills provide vistas of many shades of green and bark-brown in spring and summer, taking on a bright mantle of ruby, topaz, and golden leaves in fall.

You'll find two impressive overlooks on this trail: one at about 0.9 mile, where a welcome bench provides an excuse to rest to take in the view of southern and eastern Monroe County. The second overlook is the reward for the steepest uphill stretch: At the end of the climb, you'll reach the Lodge at Woodcliff, where you can stand higher than the treetops to look west at the distant Rochester city skyline. From here, it's clear that this county has a high concentration of natural spaces as well as a thriving populace, as dense clusters of woodland break up the expanse of residences and commercial enterprise. This view is especially magnificent on a crisp, blue-sky fall afternoon.

Miles and Directions

0.0 The trail begins at the Garnsey Road parking lot. Follow the orange blazes across the field to the woods (left of the lot), across the footbridge, and into a shrubby wooded area. The trail begins a gradual incline.

0.2 A short trail goes right here to Nancy's Glen. Turn right and follow the white blazes to this pretty tribute park, in remembrance of Nancy Whitcombe, one of the charter members of the Crescent Trail Association. When you're ready, return up the short path to the main trail and continue straight.

0.3 After a short descent, you'll cross the bridge over an unnamed stream. The trail levels out for a short time. In about 250 feet, you'll reach another bridge, after which the trail begins to climb significantly.

0.4 An old trail goes left here—continue straight. This side trail was created in the 1990s to skirt some storm debris; it's no longer used.

0.5 You've climbed about 110 feet to reach this elevation. There's a double orange blaze here; turn right. Almost immediately the trail heads downward to the stream. Start following the stream.

0.6 Turn left at the Allan's Walk sign and cross the bridge.

0.8 Turn right at the double orange blaze.

0.9 Here's another double orange blaze; continue straight ahead to the bench. Stop and take in the view. To continue on the trail, pass the bench and go down the hill, where the Orange Trail continues left. It soon meets with the Blue Trail and an unmarked trail that goes right. Turn left and continue on the Orange Trail.

1.1 Congratulations! You've just climbed the most challenging hill on this hike, with an elevation change of about 278 feet from the beginning of the trail. Turn right on the Orange Trail.

1.2 There's a dip in the trail here, at an old cut used when the lumber industry worked this hill. In about 230 feet, the trail breaks out of the woods into the maintenance yard for the Lodge at Woodcliff, the hotel on the hilltop. Cross the yard along the edge of the woods and reenter the woods when you see the wooden post with a double orange blaze. As you enter the woods, the trail turns left and starts downhill.

1.3 Here is your first junction with the Blue (return) Trail. For the moment, pass this junction and continue straight, until you leave the woods and come to the Woodcliff overlook at the top of Horizon Hill.

1.4 Here is the overlook. To the northwest, you can see the distant Rochester city skyline; to the south, the panoramic view stretches all the way to the Bristol Hills in New York's southern tier. When you're ready, return on the Orange Trail to the blue junction you passed earlier.

1.5 Turn left onto the Blue Trail.

1.6 The Red Trail joins the Blue Trail here. Continue straight on the Blue Trail. You'll pass a junction with an unmarked trail; continue on blue.

1.8 Cross a bridge here. In about 250 feet, turn left at the double blue blaze (the Red Trail goes right).

1.9 You've emerged from the woods into the field near the parking area. Turn left and continue to the trailhead.

2.1 Arrive back at the trailhead and the end of your loop.

20 Auburn Trail: Railroad Mills Special Environmental Area

The concentration of birds and butterflies on this brief section of the 9-mile Auburn Trail inspires passionate community defense of this unusual area. Bring your binoculars and plan to spend some quality time—this wilderness microcosm delivers on its promise of active wildlife.

Distance: 1.8-mile out-and-back

Approximate hiking time: 40 minutes

Difficulty: Easy

Trail surface: Narrow dirt path

Best season: April through November

Other trail users: Birders, cross-country skiers

Canine compatibility: Dogs permitted on leash

Fees and permits: None

Schedule: Open daily dawn to dusk

Maps: National Geographic Topo! New York & New Jersey

Water availability: None; drinking from the creek is not recommended

Trail contact: Town of Victor Parks and Recreation, 85 East Main Street, Victor 14564; (585) 924-1840; www.victorny.com/government/towngovernment/departments/parksrecreation; also www.saveauburntrail.org.

Special considerations: The trail is kept deliberately narrow to afford maximum habitat; this may change based on results of current studies.

Finding the trailhead: From Interstate 490 East, take exit 28 for Highway 96. Turn right at the end of the ramp, and in 0.7 mile, turn left at Fishers Road. Pass Woolston Road and bear right at the Y intersection, continuing on Fishers Road to Railroad Mills Road. Stay on Fishers, and continue down the hill past Burroughs Audubon and up the other side of the hill to the parking lot and trailhead. GPS: N43 01.599' / W77 28.947'

The Hike

Here in the heart of the Irondequoit Creek valley, the Auburn Trail reveals the ancient bed of the original Genesee River, which flowed through here for millions of years until the arrival of the last ice age. When glaciers rearranged the geology of what would become upstate New York, the ice sheets and their debris displaced the river, leaving only the slim channel of Irondequoit Creek and a broad floodplain as evidence that the Genesee had been here.

Along this geologically fascinating 0.7 mile, you can see the remarkably detailed floodplain and rolling hills—more of the glacial moraine that you see throughout northern Monroe County—that extend beyond this slender corridor. The deliberately narrow path is barely a foot wide to maximize habitat for the outstanding diversity of bird and animal life found here, but we may see some change in this configuration over the next few years as local controversy over the trail reaches a conclusion.

In the meantime, you can enjoy a wildlife walk along this path at any time of year, as birds and animals are attracted by the berry-laden trees and shrubs, wild grape, and flowering dogwoods that line the trail. Both willow and alder flycatcher are known to nest here, as well as yellow-throated vireo, Baltimore oriole, indigo bunting, and Virginia rail, to name just a few of the colorful species you may find on a spring walk. No fewer than thirty-seven butterfly species have been sighted here as well; for a complete list, visit www.saveauburntrail.org/butterflies.

All of upstate New York's most prevalent mammals can be seen here: gray squirrel, raccoon, eastern chipmunk, red fox, eastern cottontail, and skunk. Beavers have been active

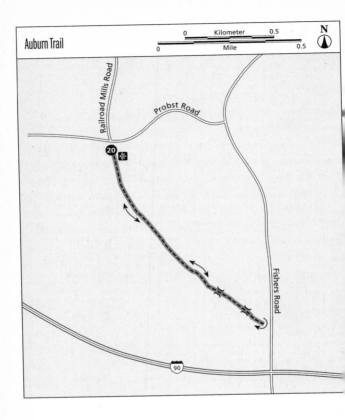

in the creek, and an occasional coyote may leave evidenc
when it passes through.

Don't feel obligated to proceed past the damaged bridg
at the south end of this trail segment; most people wh
come to bird or butterfly here stop at the creek and tur
back. The wildlife sightings tend to concentrate before th
bridge, so you may want to spend your time in this sho
trail segment.

Miles and Directions

0.0 The trailhead is at the corner of Probst and Railroad Mills Roads in Victor. Park here in one of the two spaces provided, or park alongside the road (pull off as far as you can). Walk south on the path.

0.2 You're walking alongside Irondequoit Creek. This is a nice spot to view the bend in the creek to your left, with little obstruction from the thick vegetation.

0.7 A damaged bridge crosses the creek here. Many people stop here to admire the creek and surrounding terrain, and then turn around and head back to the trailhead. If you continue across the bridge, there's another creek crossing shortly, as the creek splits in this area.

0.8 Here is the second creek crossing. Note that the land to the northeast is private property; continue straight on the trail.

0.9 You've reached Fishers Road, and the turning point for this hike. The Auburn Trail continues to the southeast. Return to the trailhead by re-crossing the creek and walking back the way you came.

1.8 Arrive back at the trailhead.

Clubs and Trail Groups

Burroughs Audubon Nature Club, P.O. Box 26814, Rochester 14626; bancny.org. This organization of nature lovers owns its own preserve near the Auburn Trail Railroad Mills section.

Crescent Trail Association, P.O. Box 1354, Fairport 14450; (585) 234-1621; www.perinton.org/Departments/RandP/hikingctha/. This is the leading organization in the development and maintenance of Perinton's trail system.

Friends of the Genesee Valley Greenway, P.O. Box 42, Mt. Morris 14510; (585) 658-2569; www.fogvg.org. Volunteers run this organization, which works tirelessly to continue development of the Greenway's remaining 35-plus miles.

Friends of Webster Trails, www.webstertrails.org. The Friends dedicate their time to maintaining and improving trails including Big Woods and Big Field, Whiting Road Nature Preserve, and several others near the lakeshore.

Genesee Valley Chapter, Adirondack Mountain Club, P.O. Box 18558, Rochester 14618; (585) 987-1717; www.gvc-adk.org. These enthusiastic hikers and conservationists schedule many outings in Monroe County and beyond throughout the year.

Genesee Valley Hiking Club, (585) 359-0902; www
.fingerlakestrail.org/gvhc.htm. Members lead many hikes—
often three in a week—from the Rochester area to the
Finger Lakes Trail in the southern tier.

Rochester Birding Association, (585) 671-1310; www
.rochesterbirding.com. For people who love seeing birds
in the wild, this organization leads several field trips every
month to find common and unusual species.

Rochester Butterfly Club, rochesterbutterflyclub.org. This
independent club promotes the study of butterflies in western New York, with field trips April through October.

Victor Hiking Trails, Inc., (585) 234-8226; www.victor
hikingtrails.org. Stewards of the Auburn Trail, sections of
the Lehigh Valley Trail, and others, this grassroots organization promotes individual responsibility for protecting the
environment.

About the Author

Randi Minetor is the author of eighteen books published by Globe Pequot Press, including three *Passport To Your National Parks Companion Guides* and *National Park Pocket Guides* to Great Smoky Mountains, Zion and Bryce Canyon, Acadia, and Everglades National Parks and Cape Cod, Assateague Island, and Gulf Islands National Seashores. Her GPP books also include three in the *Timeline Tours* series—The Battle of Gettysburg, The Battle of Fredericksburg, and Washington, D.C.—and three *Best Easy Day Hikes* FalconGuides to Buffalo, Syracuse, and Albany. Her husband, Nic Minetor, is the photographer for her *Pocket Guides* and *Timeline Tours* books. Randi is also the National Parks Examiner on Examiner.com. She and Nic live in Rochester.